60 DAYS OF UNUSUAL

RYAN LeSTRANGE

Most Charisma House Book Group products are available at special quantity discounts for bulk purchase for sales promotions, premiums, fund-raising, and educational needs. For details, call us at (407) 333-0600 or visit our website at www.charismahouse.com.

60 Days of Unusual by Ryan LeStrange
Published by Charisma House
Charisma Media/Charisma House Book Group
600 Rinehart Road, Lake Mary, Florida 32746

Unless otherwise noted, all quoted definitions are from *Merriam-Webster*, https://www.merriam-webster.com.

Unless otherwise noted, all Scripture quotations are from the New American Standard Bible, copyright © 1960, 1962, 1963, 1968, 1971, 1972, 1973, 1975, 1977, 1995 by The Lockman Foundation. Used by permission. www.Lockman.org

Scripture quotations marked AMP are from the Amplified Bible. Copyright © 2015 by The Lockman Foundation. Used by permission. www.Lockman.org

Scripture quotations marked KJV are from the King James Version of the Bible.

Visit the author's website at www.ryanlestrange.com.

Library of Congress Cataloging-in-Publication Data

Names: LeStrange, Ryan, author.
Title: 60 days of unusual / by Ryan LeStrange.
Other titles: Sixty days of unusual
Description: Lake Mary, Florida : Charisma House, 2020. | Includes
bibliographical references.
Identifiers: LCCN 2019041206 (print) | LCCN 2019041207 (ebook) | ISBN
9781629996714 (hardcover) | ISBN 9781629996721 (ebook)
Subjects: LCSH: Miracles. | Supernatural.
Classification: LCC BT97 .L4245 2020 (print) | LCC BT97 (ebook) | DDC
231.7/3--dc23
LC record available at https://lccn.loc.gov/2019041206
LC ebook record available at https://lccn.loc.gov/2019041207

While the author has made every effort to provide accurate internet addresses at the time of publication, neither the publisher nor the author assumes any responsibility for errors or for changes that occur after publication. Further, the publisher does not have any control over and does not assume any responsibility for author or third-party websites or their content.

20 21 22 23 24—987654321
Printed in the United States of America

DEDICATION

This book is dedicated to every dreamer and kingdom builder! You were not born for the ordinary. God has designed you to believe for the impossible and reach for the supernatural. May you continue to reach higher in both prayer and pursuit. May you embark on daring journeys of faith. May you pray God-sized prayers, and may you think audacious thoughts of victory and exploits. No matter what—don't let go of the dream that is in your heart.

CONTENTS

FOREWORD

For the L*ORD* *will rise up as at Mount Perazim, He will be stirred up as in the valley of Gibeon, to do His task, His* unusual *task, and to work His work, His extraordinary work.*

—ISAIAH 28:21, EMPHASIS ADDED

It is God's desire that we all experience the unusual in our lives. This can come through prophecy, preaching, prayer, the laying on of hands, and so much more. But you must believe for and expect the unusual to become a reality in your life.

Ryan LeStrange has experienced supernatural and unusual miracles in his ministry, and in this book he provides a wealth of insight into what God is speaking in this hour. It contains right-now words, definitions, and confessions that will empower you to walk in extraordinary power. If you want to see miracles, signs, and wonders, this book is for you.

There are many mysteries that God desires to make known to His people, and what Ryan reveals in these pages will lead you to breakthrough and victory. As you join Ryan on this sixty-day journey, I prophesy unusual manifestations in your personal life, family, and business. May unusual favor and unusual miracles manifest in your life today!

—John Eckhardt, Overseer, Crusaders Ministries
best-selling author, *Prayers that Rout Demons*

ACKNOWLEDGMENTS

Special thanks to my bride of over twenty years, Joy LeStrange. You have been with me through every up and down, every adventure, and every valley! Our love only grows with time. I couldn't do all that I do without you.

Thank you to my strong and amazing mother, Eileen Hromin, who has been a major part of my writing success. And I so appreciate my ministry partners, staff members, and collective team—you have blessed my life in innumerable ways! It truly takes a team and I could not do this without you. Thank you from the bottom of my heart. Let's keep adventuring together.

INTRODUCTION

I WAS RECENTLY FLYING into a particular city to minister when the Lord began to speak to me. While I was on the plane, I heard the Lord say, "Ryan, one word can change your life!" I had heard this statement many times. As a matter of fact, I have preached on this very subject. It was not new information to me, but that day when God spoke those words, they shot off in my spirit like a rocket! I felt the power of God in His decree. One word is enough to open avenues of favor. One word is enough to bring about a turnaround. One word is enough to shake things up in your life.

I began to meditate on what the Lord was saying to me. Was there one word He wanted to bring to my attention? Why had He spoken this as I was flying into that city? I asked Him, and He clearly spoke the word *unusual.* He said, "When you land, I want you to preach on the unusual. Prepare the hearts of My people for unusual and uncommon breakthroughs. Prepare them for unusual interruptions in mundane patterns in their lives. Prepare them for unusual measures of My supernatural power."

When I released the word in that service, the congregation began to report unusual breakthroughs, shifts, and blessings. Then the Lord visited me again with the same word, and this time its significance hit me even harder. I realized that although the word was extremely simple, it had a huge potential to shift lives. At the next service where I ministered, there was an explosive anointing and move of God when I declared the unusual over the congregation. People were healed and strengthened and reported making strategic decisions or experiencing a supernatural shift.

I believe God wants to do the same thing as you read this book. The word *unusual* means "not usual: uncommon, rare." Synonyms include *abnormal*, *atypical*, *uncustomary*, *especial*, *extraordinary*, *peculiar*, and *unique*.[1] That is what I believe God wants to manifest in your life as you read this book—some abnormal, atypical, uncustomary, extraordinary things!

In the Book of Acts there was a tremendous movement of unusual miracles.

> And God wrought special miracles by the hands of Paul: so that from his body were brought unto the sick handkerchiefs or aprons, and the diseases departed from them, and the evil spirits went out of them.
>
> —Acts 19:11–12, kjv

In this passage we see that a rare and uncommon dimension of God's power was bringing miraculous results. A miracle can be defined as a divine intervention in human affairs. God wants to bring miraculous results to the lives of His people. Healing miracles are one part of the equation, but I believe God wants His power to penetrate every area of your life.

Over the next sixty days we are going on a journey of reflection, meditation, and expectation based upon one word:

unusual! Prepare yourself to receive unusual blessings, walk in unusual favor, experience an unusual presence of God, and enjoy unusual insight. My prayer is that as you read each devotion and declare the confessions each day, you will expect the promise spoken to manifest in your life and thereby leave the realm of limitation and leap forward into the uncommon!

You were not born again to just live a mediocre life void of the power of God. You were created with the full nature of God on the inside of you and strategically designed to do kingdom exploits. It takes a bold plunge into the power of God to break the hold of the average and embrace the possibilities of the supernatural. So let's dive in!

UNUSUAL MIRACLES

You are the God who works wonders; You have made known Your strength among the peoples.

—Psalm 77:14

DEFINITION

Miracle—"an extraordinary event manifesting divine intervention in human affairs"; "an extremely outstanding or unusual event, thing, or accomplishment"

DEVOTION

Miracles are supernatural, divine interventions in human affairs. Miracles are not just for those in biblical days or for a rare few in modern times. God wants to intervene in your life.

Expect miracles today! Refuse to be limited by your own human thinking or natural abilities. I declare that this is a day of uncommon, miracle-working power in your life. When the power of God begins to move, the impossible becomes suddenly possible. Choose to believe God today to perform what seems to be impossible in your life.

Take the limits off! Don't limit your thinking. Don't limit your faith. Don't limit your prayers. You are not living under a closed heaven. You are living under an open heaven where the Holy Spirit has easy access into your life because of the shed blood of Jesus Christ. He came to make a way for you.

Miracles are your inheritance. Expect divine infusions of strength and power in your life today.

CONFESSION

Father, I choose to take the limits off You! I take the limits off my thinking, my dreaming, and my believing. I believe that Your power is moving in my mind, body, finances, and relationships today. I claim Your miracle-working power over my life in Jesus' name. Amen.

JOURNAL

What is God speaking to you about this prophetic promise?

DAY 2

UNUSUAL BREAKTHROUGH

Out of my distress I called on the Lord*; the* Lord *answered me and set me free.*

—Psalm 118:5, AMP

DEFINITION

Breakthrough—"an act or instance of moving through or beyond an obstacle"; "an offensive military assault that penetrates and carries beyond a defensive line"; "a sudden advance"

DEVOTION

God has appointed unusual levels of breakthrough for you. No matter how the odds seem stacked against you, the power to advance is at your disposal! As you pray, praise, and stand in faith on God's Word, the power of God is coming to your defense. You will not be held back; you will be set free! Demonic powers do their best to confine and limit, but the power of God brings freedom.

The Bible says that where the Spirit of the Lord is, there is liberty (2 Cor. 3:17). This means the presence of God brings breakthrough. The children of Israel always sent the praisers out into battle ahead of the rest of the company because the sounds of praise and thanksgiving tore down the obstacles of the enemy. Today, give God praise for your freedom. Even before the answer manifests, give Him praise for the victory. Give Him praise for an unusual advance! I decree that this is a day of freedom in every area of your life.

CONFESSION

Thank You, Father, for unusual breakthrough in every area of my life. I break all limitations, and I give You praise for uncommon levels of freedom. I decree freedom in my mind, my family, my finances, and my spiritual life. I declare that I am free! The Son has set me free, and I am free indeed. Breakthrough belongs to me in the name of Jesus. Amen.

JOURNAL

What is God speaking to you about this prophetic promise?

UNUSUAL ANOINTING

You know of Jesus of Nazareth, how God anointed Him with the Holy Spirit and with power, and how He went about doing good and healing all who were oppressed by the devil, for God was with Him.

—Acts 10:38

DEFINITION

Anointing—God's super on your natural; the difference maker in your life; the manifestation of the strength of God

DEVOTION

During His earthly ministry, Jesus was known for His extraordinary power. Wherever He went, He walked in uncommon strength and anointing. The sick were healed, the bound were set free, and the weary were refreshed—all because of the anointing.

The word translated "anointing" in Acts 10:38 is *chriō*, and it means "to smear or rub with oil."[1] When the anointing is on you, you have God's power smeared down and rubbed upon you, and you are empowered to do great exploits.

Today, God wants to release an unusual anointing upon you to assist you, strengthen you, and empower you to do kingdom exploits. Expect Him to move. When unusual levels of anointing manifest in your life, there are uncommon results.

Receive His anointing! Expect His anointing! Declare His anointing, and walk in that burden-removing power.

CONFESSION

I decree that I am anointed! God's smeared-down, rubbed-upon power is upon me. The anointing is flowing from my innermost being, and I have the anointing of God with me everywhere I go. I am strong and not weak. I walk in supernatural ability and function in the realm of the Spirit. In Jesus' name, amen.

JOURNAL

What is God speaking to you about this prophetic promise?

UNUSUAL ASSIGNMENTS

Commit your works to the LORD and
your plans will be established.
—PROVERBS 16:3

DEFINITION

Assignment—"the act of assigning something"; "a position, post, or office to which one is assigned"; "a specified task or amount of work assigned or undertaken as if assigned by authority"

DEVOTION

As you commit your steps to the Lord, He is going to send you on unusual kingdom assignments. Divine opportunities unlock supernatural ability. As you move under the direction of heaven, you will experience favor and the anointing. Lean in and listen for the instructions. Pay special attention to that small, inward leading of the Holy Spirit, and be quick to move at the slightest whispers of heaven.

A man or woman who is yielded to God can be trusted with unique tasks. Divine assignments are a vital part of this journey into the unusual. The Father has things for you to do that expand the kingdom on earth. Whether you're influencing your family, the marketplace, a relationship, or a church or ministry, your mandate is to be an effective ambassador of the kingdom in every facet of your life. Don't be shocked when you are drafted for an unusual and supernatural assignment!

CONFESSION

I thank You, Father, that my path is already established in Your love. I rest in You today. I rest in Your goodness and faithfulness, knowing that You have my steps all mapped out. I thank You for the unusual and powerful kingdom assignments in my life, and I confess that I will be quick to step out when I hear Your voice. I also confess that I have all the resources and ability to do whatever You ask me to do. I lean into You and tap into Your unusual power for the unusual assignments, in Jesus' name. Amen.

JOURNAL

What is God speaking to you about this prophetic promise?

DAY 5

UNUSUAL MOMENTS

Immediately the flow of her blood was dried up; and she felt in her body that she was healed of her affliction.

—MARK 5:29

DEFINITION

Moment—a snapshot of time; a small slice of eternity that holds potential and power

DEVOTION

God is bringing unusual moments into your life. When the woman with the issue of blood in Mark 5 heard about Jesus, she pressed through the crowd to touch Him, and she was healed as a result (vv. 25–34). But before she received her miracle, there was a moment during which she felt compelled to get up!

What if she had just sat there and accepted what was effectively a death sentence? Her story would have ended very differently. But instead of wallowing in her pain, the woman discerned the potential of the moment before her. This was a *kairos* time—God's appointed time for her healing, a moment ripe with potential and power—so she arose.

Ecclesiastes 3 tells us there is a time for everything. There are moments when you must arise, there are moments when you must be still, and there are moments that reveal the greatness that has been in you all along. God is bringing unusual moments of opportunity to you. David had a moment to defeat Goliath, and his fearless obedience to seize that moment launched him into a new season.

A moment properly discerned can unlock a new season! See and seize the moment.

CONFESSION

Father, I thank You for the powerful and profound moments in my life. I confess that I rightly discern the moment and arise as needed. I confess that I move in the power of God in my moment. I decree unusual moments of breakthrough, favor, success, and opportunity in Jesus' name. Amen.

JOURNAL

What is God speaking to you about this prophetic promise?

DAY 6

UNUSUAL CONTRACTS AND BENEFACTORS

But you shall remember the LORD your God, for it is He who is giving you power to make wealth, that He may confirm His covenant which He swore to your fathers, as it is this day.

—DEUTERONOMY 8:18

DEFINITION

Contract—"a binding agreement between two or more parties"; a commitment

Benefactor—"someone or something that provides help or an advantage: one that confers a benefit; *especially*: a person who makes a gift or bequest"

DEVOTION

Expect unusual contracts, agreements, opportunities, and wealth creation. Deuteronomy 8:18 promises power to generate wealth and declares an anointing for increase. God wants to bring you before people who will be a part of your turnaround and give you favor with them. Expect this by faith. God is giving you the ability to enlarge and expand.

Unusual opportunities are coming to you. Unusual deals are coming to you. I can still remember the first major publishing contract I received. It was a promise fulfilled, but I had prayed for it, declared it, and believed for it before it ever came. Your faith opens the doorway for enlargement.

CONFESSION

Father, I thank You for unusual opportunities, contracts, and benefactors. You are bringing me before the right people with the right opportunities that will enable me to accomplish Your plans for my life. I decree unusual dimensions of increase over my life in Jesus' name. Amen!

JOURNAL

What is God speaking to you about this prophetic promise?

UNUSUAL PARTNERSHIPS, CONNECTIONS, AND ALIGNMENTS

Two are better than one because they have a good return for their labor. For if either of them falls, the one will lift up his companion. But woe to the one who falls when there is not another to lift him up.

—Ecclesiastes 4:9–10

DEFINITION

Partnership—"a relationship resembling a legal partnership and usually involving close cooperation between parties having specified and joint rights and responsibilities"

Connection—a link or bond between people, businesses, or ministries

Alignment—"the act of aligning or state of being aligned; *especially*: the proper positioning or state of adjustment of parts (as of a mechanical or electronic device) in relation to each other"; "a forming in line"; "an arrangement of groups or forces in relation to one another"

DEVOTION

Don't be shocked by unusual partnerships and alignments. A major part of destiny is the "who" we end up connecting with. We often get extremely focused on the "what" and the "where," but we forget that who we do life, destiny, and kingdom exploits with makes a tremendous difference.

Expect divine connections. Be quick to recognize momentum in relationships and sow into them. In the busyness of life it is extremely easy to overlook kingdom connections. Be sensitive to the open doors God brings and the way He connects you with the right people. Who God chooses to connect you with may shock you. Many times, when you are about to enter a new season, there will be new relationships or the deepening of current ones. There may also be a release from some old relationships. Let God send the unusual connections and partnerships into your life. Two are better than one!

CONFESSION

Father, I thank You for glorious and divine connections in my life. I expect right alignments and kingdom relationships. I expect supernatural partnerships in my life. I decree that You are connecting me to the right people and disconnecting me from the wrong people, in Jesus' name. Amen.

JOURNAL

What is God speaking to you about this prophetic promise?

DAY 8

UNUSUAL BOLDNESS

Wait for the LORD; be strong and let your heart take courage; yes, wait for the LORD.

—PSALM 27:14

DEFINITION

Bold—"fearless before danger"

DEVOTION

God is releasing unusual boldness to you! In order to do what God has called you to do, you must not be afraid. To embark on kingdom exploits, you must be delivered from fear. God is giving you audacious dreams. He is looking for men and women who dare to abandon limited thinking, believing, and praying. Heaven is looking for men and women to whom the Father can download earth-shaking dreams.

Boldness is linked with courage. The enemy does all he can to sow fear into your life. He gets you thinking on the wrong things, speaking the wrong things, and believing the wrong things. Spend time in the presence of God, and allow Him to fill your heart with His strong love, which brings reassurance and courage. As He gives you uncommon vision, He will release uncommon boldness so you can step out into the realm of miracles.

CONFESSION

Father, I thank You for Your boldness in my life. I thank You that You have not given me a spirit of fear but of power, love, and a sound mind. I decree courage in my life. I decree strength in my life. I decree bravery to take the plunge and execute the will of God in my life, in Jesus' name. Amen.

JOURNAL

What is God speaking to you about this prophetic promise?

UNUSUAL GENIUS

For who has known the mind of the LORD, that he will instruct Him? But we have the mind of Christ.
—1 CORINTHIANS 2:16

DEFINITION

Genius—"extraordinary intellectual power especially as manifested in creative activity"; "a person endowed with extraordinary mental superiority"

DEVOTION

Genius is exceptional intellectual or creative power or other natural ability. It is brilliance, intelligence, intellect, ability, and cleverness. It is not common! Imagine tapping the realm of unlimited insight, wisdom, and knowledge! It is available. Uncommon genius is accessible to you for all of life's decisions and challenges. Realms of uncommon creative power and ability are available to you. It's time to believe for and tap into the limit-breaking power of God's wisdom.

God is releasing unusual and exceptional ideas, plans, and strategies for you. Tap into the mind of Christ through prayer, confession, and meditation. Refuse to limit your thinking, your dreams, or your imagination. Let God loose in your thinking, and choose to seek His mind concerning every situation you face.

CONFESSION

Thank You, Lord, for releasing unusual genius in my life. I confess that Your creativity and wisdom are manifesting in my life. I decree life-changing strategies and ideas be released. Thank You, Father, for giving me the mind of Christ. I confess that I walk in wisdom and divine solutions, in the name of Jesus. Amen.

JOURNAL

What is God speaking to you about this prophetic promise?

UNUSUAL PROTECTION

For He will give His angels charge concerning you, to guard you in all your ways. They will bear you up in their hands, that you do not strike your foot against a stone.

—PSALM 91:11–12

DEFINITION

Protection—"the act of protecting: the state of being protected"; preservation from injury or harm; a thing, person, or group that protects; in the biblical sense, abiding under the canopy of heaven and separated from the enemy

DEVOTION

Expect unusual protection. This is one of the most beautiful attributes of the Father's love for you. He protects you. He has provided supernatural protection for your mind, body, and life. You do not have to be afraid of the plots of the enemy.

God's hand can rescue you from calamity, tragedy, and accidents. It is vital that you learn to rest in His unusual protection for you. As you hear His voice and follow His leading, He will guide you away from danger, whether it be physical or spiritual. Trust the voice of the Lord, and believe for His protection.

CONFESSION

Father, I thank You for protecting me and my family. I place all that I have in Your hands. I break the power of fear off my life in the name of Jesus. I rebuke every spirit of fear, accidents, calamity, and exploitation. I rest in You. I am secure in You. I hear Your voice and obey. You are my safe place. I thank You for unusual and supernatural protection, in Jesus' name. Amen.

JOURNAL

What is God speaking to you about this prophetic promise?

DAY 11

UNUSUAL *SHAMAR*

I have set watchmen upon thy walls, O Jerusalem, which shall never hold their peace day nor night: ye that make mention of the L*ORD*, *keep not silence.*

—ISAIAH 62:6, KJV

DEFINITION

Shamar—to watch, guard, keep, be a watchman[1]

Guard—"To protect, to watch over, to stand guard over, to police, to secure, to defend, to shield, to shelter, to screen, to cover, to cloak, to preserve, to save, to conserve, to supervise, to keep under surveillance or control, to keep under guard, to govern, to restrain, to suppress, to keep watch, to be alert, or to take care"[2]

DEVOTION

One dimension of the prophetic anointing is the *shamar* dimension. This is when you experience a watchman anointing to protect your life. Expect an unusual level of *shamar*! Heaven is going to shine light on the plans of the enemy and those coming to deceive or bring you harm.

Be quick to obey a nudge from Holy Spirit to do something or *not* to do something. There are many ways you can receive a warning. It can come through the voice of God, a vision or dream, an impression, or even your spiritual senses.

Sometimes you do not know where it is coming from; you just have a sense not to move in a particular direction.

Your spirit man has an internal warning system. Don't ignore its caution signals.

CONFESSION

Father, I thank You for giving me the ability to watch and pray. I pause, ponder, meditate, and listen. I need Your warnings in my life, and I expect an uncommon level of shamar *in my life. I am determined not to miss it. I am determined not to be deceived or sidetracked. I am determined to follow Holy Spirit every step of the way. Thank You for Your guidance and protection, in Jesus' name. Amen.*

JOURNAL

What is God speaking to you about this prophetic promise?

UNUSUAL INSIGHT

That the God of our Lord Jesus Christ, the Father of glory, may give to you a spirit of wisdom and of revelation in the knowledge of Him. I pray that the eyes of your heart may be enlightened, so that you will know what is the hope of His calling, what are the riches of the glory of His inheritance in the saints, and what is the surpassing greatness of His power toward us who believe. These are in accordance with the working of the strength of His might.

—EPHESIANS 1:17–19

DEFINITION

Insight—"the power or act of seeing into a situation"; "the act or result of apprehending the inner nature of things or of seeing intuitively";[1] "the capacity to gain an accurate and deep intuitive understanding of a person or thing";[2] synonyms include "intuition, discernment, perception, awareness, understanding, comprehension, apprehension, appreciation, penetration, acumen, perspicacity, judgment, acuity"[3]

DEVOTION

Paul prayed for the church at Ephesus to have unusual revelation. This is one of the keys to successful kingdom living: to clearly hear, see, and know. When you walk in unusual insight, you will have explosive results. Your path will become clearer. Your strategy will be stronger and your steps surer.

Wisdom, mysteries, and revelation are available to you as a born-again believer. They are not reserved for those who walk in the office of the prophet. You also have a prophetic nature. The prophetic anointing you have been given allows you access to uncommon understanding. It enables you to "look beyond" and see the thing behind a thing. Expect unusual insight and revelation.

CONFESSION

Father, I thank You that the eyes of my inner man are enlightened. I thank You that I have the spirit of wisdom and revelation. I declare that I walk in extraordinary insight, in the name of Jesus. Amen.

JOURNAL

What is God speaking to you about this prophetic promise?

DAY 13

UNUSUAL DISCERNMENT

For nothing is hidden that will not become evident, nor anything secret that will not be known and come to light.

—LUKE 8:17

DEFINITION

Discern—"to detect with senses other than vision"

DEVOTION

Discernment is the ability to look beyond. This gift is vital to the believer because we must be able to see through the eyes of the Spirit and determine the will of God in a given situation. Some may think this gift is reserved for a select few, but Paul taught in 1 Corinthians 12 that the discerning of spirits is available to all believers as we are led by the Spirit of God. It was not given only to the elite. It is accessible to every person who has been born again.

The discerning of spirits is the ability to see the spirit motivating a person or situation. It cuts through the clutter and gets to the root. Make no mistake: motives matter. The right action with the wrong motive can be toxic. But God can reveal to you the motives influencing a person or situation. Unusual discernment is yours as you press into the mind and heart of God. This is part of His promise to lead you by His Spirit.

CONFESSION

Father, I thank You for giving me uncommon discernment. I boldly confess that the nine gifts of the Spirit are my inheritance. I have free access to the gifts of God. I decree that the discerning of spirits functions fully in my life. I see and hear correctly. I will not be deceived or misled by a person with impure motives. I am submitted and committed to Your will, in Jesus' name. Amen.

JOURNAL

What is God speaking to you about this prophetic promise?

UNUSUAL PRAYER

And said unto them, It is written, My house shall be called the house of prayer.

—MATTHEW 21:13, KJV

DEFINITION

Prayer—intimate time with the Father

DEVOTION

One of God's greatest desires is for His people to commune with Him. Prayer is many things, but at its heart it is simply intimate time with the Father. In prayer, battles are won, victories secured, and storms turned back. Prayer releases strategies, dispatches angels, and unveils heavenly plans. That is why prayer must become a lifestyle.

Unusual desire and dedication to prayer is coming forth in your life. You will be drawn to the presence of God. You will find yourself awakened to pray. An uncommon longing for the presence of God is a catalyst for life-altering blessings. You will find yourself praying throughout the day as the Father creates a hunger in you for His presence.

CONFESSION

Father, I love Your presence. I decree an anointing to pray over my life. I declare that I am drawn to the secret place with You. I break distractions off my life in the name of Jesus. I call forth the fire of prayer and a passion for Your presence. I thank You, Lord, for giving me an appetite for communion and spending quiet time with You. Thank You for sweetly drawing me to the place of prayer in Jesus' name. Amen.

JOURNAL

What is God speaking to you about this prophetic promise?

UNUSUAL HUNGER

O God, You are my God; I shall seek You earnestly; my soul thirsts for You, my flesh yearns for You, in a dry and weary land where there is no water.

—Psalm 63:1

DEFINITION

Hunger—"a strong desire"; "a craving or urgent need for food or a specific nutrient"; "a weakened condition brought about by prolonged lack"; a painful sensation or state of weakness caused by the need for something

DEVOTION

Pursuit is key to accessing the supernatural realm, and hunger causes us to pursue. Therefore, hunger causes us to access power.

Uncommon hunger will become a catalyst for seeking. At our core we are created to seek God, and our first call is to His presence. What we will find in His presence cannot be found anywhere else. Our hunger for Him connects us to all that is meaningful.

Those who do not have a revelation of God's presence will deem our pursuit of Him meaningless, but you and I, who are expecting God to do the unusual, have a different perspective. We will gladly pour ourselves out at His feet. We will give countless moments to Him just to experience His presence. In the most difficult times it is His presence that resets us and reestablishes our hearts in hope. God is releasing unusual hunger for Himself in our hearts because hunger is the key that opens massive doors to encounter and breakthrough.

CONFESSION

Lord, thank You for igniting in my heart a burning hunger for You. I declare that I want Your presence, Your glory, and Your power in my life. I am a God-seeker. I refuse to be distracted, in the name of Jesus. I decree that I am focused in prayer, focused in worship, and committed to pursuit. Thank You, Lord, for causing me to wake up thinking about You and go to sleep thinking about You. Thank You, Lord, for causing me to have unusual hunger for You in the name of Jesus. Amen.

JOURNAL

What is God speaking to you about this prophetic promise?

UNUSUAL SEEKING

When he heard that it was Jesus the Nazarene, he began to cry out and say, "Jesus, Son of David, have mercy on me!" Many were sternly telling him to be quiet, but he kept crying out all the more, "Son of David, have mercy on me!"...And Jesus said to him, "Go; your faith has made you well." Immediately he regained his sight and began following Him on the road.

—MARK 10:47–48, 52

DEFINITION

Seek—"to go in search of"; "to ask for: request"; "to try to acquire or gain";[1] "to try to find or discover by searching or questioning"[2]

DEVOTION

In Mark 10 blind Bartimaeus caught Jesus' attention and received a life-changing miracle. The story intrigues me because we see clearly that his seeking initiated the breakthrough. In a moment a lifetime of bondage was broken.

In this account we see the power of pursuit. When we pursue Jesus, we move far beyond the confines of both demonic bondage and human limitation. We advance into the miracle realm.

Unusual seeking will cause a person to rise up early and

stay up late. A person who is seeking something will spend countless hours in pursuit of it. If the individual is seeking knowledge, he will read books, attend conferences, and travel great distances.

I believe God wants to inspire uncommon pursuit in your life. He wants to awaken your heart to the possibilities and create a place for faith, hunger, tenacity, and unusual seeking.

CONFESSION

Father, I thank You for the power of pursuit in my life. I declare that I love to seek Your face and that I am a person of prayer, passion, and encounter. I love Your presence and value spending time with You. I expect unusual miracle encounters and breakthrough as I devote myself to seeking You. In the name of Jesus, amen.

JOURNAL

What is God speaking to you about this prophetic promise?

UNUSUAL FAITH

Now faith is the assurance (title deed, confirmation) of things hoped for (divinely guaranteed), and the evidence of things not seen [the conviction of their reality—faith comprehends as fact what cannot be experienced by the physical senses].

–HEBREWS 11:1, AMP

DEFINITION

Faith—to believe beyond your natural senses. Abraham believed according to what God said, not according to how he felt (Rom. 4:16–21). True faith is based on God's promise and not what we see or feel.

DEVOTION

Uncommon faith creates an avenue for uncommon answers, breakthroughs, solutions, and miracles. Faith releases you from the natural realm and creates a point of access for the realm of the spirit in your life. As you walk by faith, you lay hold of the promises of God. Faith believes God and takes Him at His word. Faith boldly claims the promises of God. Faith speaks it! Faith stands on it! Faith does not waver. Because faith pleases God, it also receives from God.

Unusual faith will bring unusual answers. Choose to take the limits off and plunge deep into God's promises. Choose to take God at His word, and know that if He said it, He meant it! Choose to drown out the doubt with God's promises. Those who walk by faith will receive answers! Their faith will not be denied. Unusual faith will forever alter your course and define your life.

CONFESSION

Father, I thank You that I walk by faith and not by sight. I believe Your promises and claim them over my life. I decree that I am strong and not weak. I decree that I am healed and whole. I decree that I boldly stand upon Your word without wavering. I am Your child, and all of Your promises to me are yes and amen. I speak to mountains, and they move! I declare the answers over the problems. I am a person of faith. My faith is alive and active, and I receive blessings and breakthroughs now in Jesus' name. Amen.

JOURNAL

What is God speaking to you about this prophetic promise?

DAY 18

UNUSUAL WORSHIP

All nations whom You have made shall come and worship before You, O Lord, and they shall glorify Your name. For You are great and do wondrous deeds; You alone are God.

—PSALM 86:9–10

DEFINITION

Worship— The Hebrew word translated "worship" in Psalm 86:9 is *shachah*. Some of its meanings are "to bow down," to "prostrate oneself," and to pay homage.[1] Worship, therefore, is a holy reverence or bowing down before a holy God. It is, at its core, an expression of thankfulness, adoration, devotion, and honor.

DEVOTION

Every person ever created was born to worship God. There is something about the intimate presence of God that brings you right back to the place of intimacy He wanted to have with us when He created mankind. His presence is healing. His presence is tender. His presence is powerful. We were born for His presence. In His presence there is peace and tranquility. In His presence there is comfort. His presence contains victory and breakthrough.

We must choose to surrender to God through worship on a daily basis. Unusual worship can bring you into higher levels of glory and power. Unusual worship can cause both individuals and groups of people to enter into levels of encounter that are rare.

CONFESSION

Thank You, Lord, that I am a worshipper. I confess that I love Your presence. I love to be with You in Your glory. I love to spend time at Your feet. I love to anoint You with my worship. I love You, Father. I was made for Your glory. My heart longs for You, and I daily seek Your face. I am a God-seeker who is in love with You, Lord.

JOURNAL

What is God speaking to you about this prophetic promise?

DAY 19

UNUSUAL PRAISE

Every day I will bless You, and I will praise Your name forever and ever.

—PSALM 145:2

DEFINITION

Praise—the offering of grateful homage to God in word or song. Looking at some of the Hebrew words translated "praise" paints a vivid picture.[1] The most common one is *halal*, which means "to make a show, to boast; and thus to be (clamorously) foolish; to rave."[2] *Yadah* means to revere or worship with one's hands extended.[3] *Barak* means "to bless."[4] *Tĕhillah* refers to a "song or hymn of praise."[5] *Zamar* refers to playing an instrument and points to praising God with music.[6] *Towdah* means to praise with a heart of thankfulness,[7] and *shabach* means to laud or praise God in a loud tone.[8]

DEVOTION

Praise is a weapon! To praise is to lift up. When you praise God, you are lifting Him up above all else. You are reminding yourself of His goodness and lifting Him up above every battle and struggle. Praise is pushing past the opposition and purposefully focusing on Jesus and all of His glory. This is why it is such a distinct and powerful discipline for a child of God.

Unusual praise sets the tone for a life of victory. Unusual praise involves making noise, lifting your hands, and aggressively thanking God for who He is and all that He has done. Unusual praise is unbothered by man's opinions and is not afraid to appear foolish. In fact, praisers are foolish in the eyes of those who rely on their own wisdom to get the job done.

A praiser is focused on God; He is number one. Praise pushes back darkness, breaks down walls, and releases heavy glory because praise invokes the life-shifting power of God.

CONFESSION

Thank You, Lord, for making me a praiser. I decree that I am taking my praise up a notch. I am going to praise You wildly and foolishly. I am going to go wholeheartedly into Your presence with no shame or fear. I say that You are great and greatly to be praised. It is an honor to spend time with You and love You, Father. Thank You for unusual praise and breakthrough in the name of Jesus. Amen.

JOURNAL

What is God speaking to you about this prophetic promise?

UNUSUAL AUTHORITY

They were amazed at His teaching; for He was teaching them as one having authority, and not as the scribes.

—MARK 1:22

DEFINITION

Authority—The Greek word translated "authority" in Mark 1:22 is *exousia.* In addition to referring to moral influence, *exousia* denotes power and is associated with having jurisdiction or dominion over a certain area as well as a right or ability.[1]

DEVOTION

Jesus taught with great authority and commanded demons to leave people. The religious crowd of that day wasn't used to those supernatural realms of deliverance. They did not know how to receive the level of authority that Jesus walked in. His ministry displaced bondages and unlocked explosive kingdom power—and this is a picture of what is available to you as a child of God!

Unusual authority breaks heaviness, releases healing, and annihilates the powers of darkness. Unusual authority combined with faith moves mountains and calms storms.

The authority of heaven legislates and mandates the full force of the kingdom. Meditate on this truth and allow it to become active in your life. God desires to bring you into dimensions of authority that unleash explosive and supernatural results.

CONFESSION

Father, I thank You that I am seated with You in heavenly places. Thank You for giving me authority over demons, sickness, and all the works of hell. I decree that I walk in unusual authority. I decree that I am Your ambassador, authorized and commissioned by You. I move in Your power and legal authority in Jesus' name. Amen.

JOURNAL

What is God speaking to you about this prophetic promise?

DAY 21

UNUSUAL STAMINA

Let us not lose heart in doing good, for in due time we will reap if we do not grow weary.

—GALATIANS 6:9

DEFINITION

Stamina—"the ability to sustain"; synonyms include "endurance, staying power...fortitude, strength...energy...toughness, determination, tenacity, perseverance."[1] People with stamina have no quitting sense. They keep going to the end of the race no matter the obstacles. They have grit.

DEVOTION

Galatians 6:9 contains a powerful prophetic picture. We will reap the harvest on the seeds we have sown, the prayers we have prayed, and the kingdom labor we have performed if we do not faint! That is God's promise to us.

So what is the role of the enemy in this equation? He wants to harass you, attack you, and wear you out. He is trying to get you to throw in the towel before the harvest comes. The enemy is determined! He has his sights set upon you. The confusion, lies, and heaviness that are currently hitting you have a clear aim—to take you out before breakthrough comes. The devil knows well the enemies of your breakthrough.

To stand in the midst of opposition, you must have

spiritual, emotional, and mental stamina. You must be able to go long and strong. Boxers have to do more than start well; they must stay in the ring, pace themselves, and keep swinging in a strategic manner. They have to outlast the enemy!

This is a picture of what you and I must do as believers. I decree that God is giving you staying power. He is protecting and securing you. He is enabling you to see His promise and be refreshed. He is appointing breakthrough for you. You will endure. *You will not quit!*

CONFESSION

I decree spiritual strength and might in my life. I decree that I am not weary but am being renewed daily. I decree that I have spiritual stamina and will not quit. I decree that I am moving from glory to glory in the name of Jesus. I say that I am strong and not weak. Thank You, Lord, for Your refreshing and glory in my life. In the name of Jesus, amen.

JOURNAL

What is God speaking to you about this prophetic promise?

UNUSUAL ATMOSPHERES

They began laughing at Him. But putting them all out, He took along the child's father and mother and His own companions, and entered the room where the child was. Taking the child by the hand, He said to her, "Talitha kum!" (which translated means, "Little girl, I say to you, get up!"). Immediately the girl got up and began to walk, for she was twelve years old. And immediately they were completely astounded.

—Mark 5:40–42

DEFINITION

Atmosphere—"a surrounding or pervading mood, environment, or influence."[1] An atmosphere contains power to change lives! A negative atmosphere brings pollution of thought and emotions, but an atmosphere of glory causes people to arise. (See Isaiah 60:1.)

DEVOTION

In the midst of the right atmosphere, miracles erupt like a volcano. When Jesus went into Jairus' house to raise his daughter from the dead, He shifted the atmosphere by kicking all the grieving people out. He knew that their grief was toxic to the parents' faith, so He strategically chose those who would go in with Him.

Atmosphere matters. One day the Lord spoke to me and said, "Expect unusual gatherings, unusual meetings, and unusual prayer gatherings." Now I declare to you to expect uncommon dimensions of God's glory to show up and work wonders. Be sensitive to those divine appointments. Be ready for the glory of God. Be ready for His miracle power by setting an unusual atmosphere of praise, prayer, worship, and hunger in your home and family. Guard the atmosphere around you. Cleanse and protect it so you can experience a new dimension of the power of God.

CONFESSION

Thank You, Lord, for giving me the desire and ability to create powerful atmospheres of breakthrough in my life. I decree that I am led by Your Spirit into Your will for my life in Jesus' name. I say that I am a glory dweller, and I love Your presence. I am drawn to glory gatherings. I am drawn to places where Your presence abides. I love and seek Your presence in Jesus' name. Amen.

JOURNAL

What is God speaking to you about this prophetic promise?

UNUSUAL CLEANSING

Create in me a clean heart, O God, and renew a steadfast spirit within me.

—PSALM 51:10

DEFINITION

Cleansing—In the biblical sense *cleansing* means to purify, make clean, or renew. It is often used instead of the words *purge* or *purify*, having the same root and meaning as the word *clean*. Don't be surprised when heaven shows up to clean out your closet, removing wrong motives, thinking, and even relationships.

DEVOTION

As you press into the realm of the supernatural and the unusual, there will be cleansing! Many times in my life when God has radically advanced me, it has caused a supernatural cleansing to occur. The cleansing does not always feel good, but it is necessary to answer your prayers. Embrace the process. Don't go through it kicking and screaming. Simply say, "God, I surrender. I surrender to Your ways, to Your plans, to Your desires. I place my life in Your hands, and I trust You."

I declare unusual cleansing in your heart, in your anointing, in your calling, and in your relationships. I release the fire of God over you to burn out the chaff and bring you into greater glory. The cleansing fire is sweeping over your life in order to position you for the mega doors that the Father wants to guide you through. You will cooperate with heaven's agenda and walk in uncommon peace through the process.

CONFESSION

I surrender all to You, Father! You are my all in all. Search my heart, Lord, and purify me. Purify my motives, my mind, and my life. I surrender totally to You. I come back to that place of absolute abandonment in Your presence and glory. You are my Father, and I am Your child. Cleanse me, O God! I want all that You have for me. In Jesus' name, amen.

JOURNAL

What is God speaking to you about this prophetic promise?

UNUSUAL GRACE

And He has said to me, "My grace is sufficient for you, for power is perfected in weakness." Most gladly, therefore, I will rather boast about my weaknesses, so that the power of Christ may dwell in me.

—2 CORINTHIANS 12:9

DEFINITION

Grace—There are so many definitions and deep meanings for the word *grace*. It is unmerited favor. It is God's goodness toward all of us who have no claim on, nor any reason to expect, divine favor. It is love; it is forgiveness; it is all that Jesus has paid for us to have.

DEVOTION

In 2 Corinthians 12 Paul came to the end of himself. He realized that everything he needed was in the total and complete work of Jesus on the cross. He understood that it was in the grace of God that his calling was complete and his identity secure. It was grace that caused Jesus to die for him while he was yet a sinner. It was grace that apprehended him on the Damascus Road. It was grace that led him to faith and to stand in the righteousness of God in Christ Jesus. It was grace that bought him. It was grace that freed him.

Unusual grace causes you to have mega mercy and

forgiveness toward others. A heart that is planted in grace is free! It is free from self-protecting, free from striving, free from torment, free from fear. God wants to release a revelation of unusual grace in you and through you to others. The revelation of His grace will set you totally free from bondage.

CONFESSION

Thank You, Lord, for Your amazing grace. I receive Your grace in my life, and I confess that I walk in love and grace toward others. I thank You, Father, for a revelation of Your goodness in my life. I thank You for an "It is finished" mindset that sets me free to soar, free to dream, free to love, and free to be! I decree that I am free. I am free indeed by Your grace. In Jesus' name, amen.

JOURNAL

What is God speaking to you about this prophetic promise?

UNUSUAL COMPASSION

Moved with compassion, Jesus touched their eyes; and immediately they regained their sight and followed Him.

—MATTHEW 20:34

DEFINITION

Compassion—the characteristic of recognizing the suffering of others and being moved to take action to help. It is what fuels acts of kindness and mercy. Love is at the core of every act of compassion. "God is love" (1 John 4:8).

DEVOTION

In Matthew 20 Jesus was leaving Jericho, and a large crowd was following Him. Along the road were two blind men, who cried out as Jesus was passing, "Lord, have mercy on us, Son of David!" (v. 30). Jesus' reaction was one of kindness and concern for the plight of these blind men. He reacted from a place of tenderness, and it brought a manifestation of God's power.

Compassion is a powerful tool in the ministry of healing. When we sense the pain of others and are tender toward them, we are unveiling an aspect of God's heart. The enemy will try to harden us so we refuse to feel or be tender, but this is not the will of God. We are not to be calloused but to be tender and vulnerable.

Unusual compassion is the gateway to prayer assignments,

prophetic assignments, and miracles. Allow the Lord to move upon your heart and touch it with compassion for others. It will unlock a flow of miracles.

CONFESSION

Father, thank You for making me sensitive to others, including their needs and desires. Thank You for causing me to be moved with compassion when there is a need, a pain, or an issue. Thank You for making my heart tender before You in the name of Jesus. Amen.

JOURNAL

What is God speaking to you about this prophetic promise?

DAY 26

UNUSUAL RESTORATION

Instead of your shame you will have a double portion, and instead of humiliation they will shout for joy over their portion. Therefore they will possess a double portion in their land, everlasting joy will be theirs.

—ISAIAH 61:7

DEFINITION

Restore—to "bring back (a previous right, practice, custom, or situation)"; "reinstate"; "return (someone or something) to a former condition, place, or position"; "repair or renovate...so as to return it to its original condition"[1]

DEVOTION

God wants to bring unusual levels of restoration in your life! He wants to show His mighty hand upon you. The enemy has done his best to tear you down, but God has good plans for you. He wants to restore promises. He wants to restore ministries. He wants to restore finances. He wants to restore health. He wants to restore relationships. God is the Restorer. His promise in Isaiah was one of massive restoration. God knows how to perform a mega turnaround.

Trust Him today for uncommon rehabilitation! He knows how to bring things back in line with His plan. Thank and praise Him for restoration. Believe Him for restoration. Believe that every area the enemy has touched will turn around. Fight the devil with the Word of the Lord. *Press in for the double!*

CONFESSION

Thank You, Lord, for turning it around. Thank You, Lord, for bringing massive restoration in my life. Thank You, Lord, for bringing supernatural rehabilitation and strength. Thank You, Lord, for scattering my enemies and arising in my life. I claim unusual restoration in Jesus' name. Amen.

JOURNAL

What is God speaking to you about this prophetic promise?

UNUSUAL HEALING

He sent His word and healed them, and delivered them from their destructions.
—PSALM 107:20

DEFINITION

Heal—"to make well again: to restore to health"; "to restore to original purity or integrity." It is always God's will for us to walk in complete health in our spirit, soul, and body.

DEVOTION

Jesus came to bring healing in every area. His sacrifice on the cross brought healing to your mind, healing to your body, and healing to your spirit. He paid the full price with His blood, and by His wounds we were healed (1 Pet. 2:24). The Bible tells us that Jesus is the same yesterday, today, and forever.

The ministry of Jesus on earth is perfect theology. Therefore, whatever we see Jesus doing in the Bible should set our standard for what we should be doing as followers of Christ. He went about healing everywhere. If sickness and defeat were of God, then Jesus was in rebellion because the Bible tells us that Jesus was born "to destroy the works of the devil" (1 John 3:8). This was one of His mandates.

Sickness and infirmity are from hell. Hell wants to make you sick, weak, and defeated. God wants to bring unusual levels of healing and miracles to your life. Begin to meditate on this. Watch videos and listen to teachings that inspire your faith in this area. Pray big, bold, and wild prayers. Instead of thinking about all the things making you sick, start thinking that you are healed! Start putting a demand on the healing ministry of Jesus in every area of your life, and watch God's power flow.

CONFESSION

Thank You, Lord, for manifesting Your healing power in my life. Thank You, Lord, for bringing healing in every area. I believe that You paid the price for me to be well, and I receive Your healing ministry in the name of Jesus. Amen.

JOURNAL

What is God speaking to you about this prophetic promise?

UNUSUAL DETERMINATION

And the Lord said, "Hear what the unrighteous judge said; now, will not God bring about justice for His elect who cry to Him day and night, and will He delay long over them? I tell you that He will bring about justice for them quickly. However, when the Son of Man comes, will He find faith on the earth?"

—LUKE 18:6–8

DEFINITION

Determination—The Greek word often translated "determine" is *krinō*, which means to resolve or decide.[1] Much like the word *stamina*, *determination* denotes a fortitude, a drive, a tenacity.

DEVOTION

In this passage in Luke 18 Jesus is teaching on prayer. He provides a powerful illustration by giving the story of a widow who continually cried out to an unjust judge. The woman was determined to have her case heard and demanded justice. She refused to give up. Despite the odds being stacked against her, the widow went before the unjust judge time and time again.

Finally the judge said to himself, "Even though I do not fear God nor respect man, yet because this widow bothers me, I will give her legal protection, otherwise by continually coming she will wear me out" (Luke 18:4–5). The story clearly shows this woman's persistence. But Jesus ended the story by tying it into faith.

Tenacity and determination are attributes of faith. Faith comes into the spirit of a man or woman when the person has clearly heard from God. Along with that faith, determination will cause a person to refuse to accept no for an answer. It will cause a person to take unusual action. Determination will cause a person to do things that are extremely inconvenient. Determination will cause a person to seek.

God is unlocking faith in your life and releasing unusual determination. As you dig into the will and plan of God for your life, you are going to be rooted and grounded. You are going to refuse to cede one piece of ground to the devil. You are going to stand boldly and firmly upon the promise…determined!

CONFESSION

Thank You, Lord, for placing an unusual determination in my life. I decree that I am not a quitter. I don't give up or give in. I stand upon the promises of God with boldness and determination. Thank You, Lord, for making me a person of uncommon faith. In Jesus' name, amen.

JOURNAL

What is God speaking to you about this prophetic promise?

DAY 29

UNUSUAL EXPECTATION

Do not let your heart envy sinners [who live godless lives and have no hope of salvation], but [continue to] live in the [reverent, worshipful] fear of the LORD day by day. Surely there is a future [and a reward], and your hope and expectation will not be cut off. Listen, my son, and be wise, and direct your heart in the way [of the LORD].

—PROVERBS 23:17–19, AMP

DEFINITION

Expect—"to consider probable or certain"; "to anticipate or look forward to the coming or occurrence of"; synonyms include "[to] hope" and "look forward to."[1] Expectation is the characteristic of faith that grabs hold of the promise.

DEVOTION

Unusual expectation provides a platform for amazing miracles and breakthroughs. Expectation creates an atmosphere where you are looking for the move of God. When you are expectant, you are anticipating something supernatural. Your heart becomes stirred, and you know that something is about to happen! This is the entryway to the miraculous realm.

I believe today that God wants to wipe out the disappointment in your heart and release unusual expectation. He wants to get you on the edge of your seat looking, waiting, and watching. He wants you to be asking, "What will come next?" This is a powerful position to be in. *You* are literally on the verge of a mega move of God. Allow your heart to soar higher into the realm of possibilities and dreaming.

CONFESSION

I thank You, Lord, that I am full of expectation! I refuse to live paralyzed by fear and doubt. I refuse to live wondering and wavering. I choose to believe You, Father. I believe Your promises, Your plans, and Your dreams for my life. I believe in Your power and miracles. I release my heart to soar in expectation in Jesus' name. Amen.

JOURNAL

What is God speaking to you about this prophetic promise?

UNUSUAL PEACE

The steadfast of mind You will keep in perfect peace, because he trusts in You.

—Isaiah 26:3

DEFINITION

Peace—*Shalowm*, the Hebrew word translated "peace," comes from the root *shalam*, which can mean to be complete or made whole.[1]

DEVOTION

There is a realm of unusual peace that is available to you. When you choose to dwell in Jesus, a blanket of peace comes upon you.

The Lord said that you can remain in peace if you keep your mind fixed upon Him. If you stay rooted in His promises, you will abort the tormenting plans of hell and live in uncommon tranquility. This is a promise not for a few select believers but for each one of us. This is what was happening when the boat was being tossed to and fro and Jesus was sleeping (Matt. 8:23–27). He was unbothered because He knew His Father. Knowing the Father on an intimate level causes your heart to be established in complete peace.

The shalom of God is His wholeness and completeness in every area of your life! He finished it. He planned it. He paid the price for you to be whole in every way. And now you get to enjoy it. His peace comes as a result of knowing who He is and choosing to remain in that truth. In that place of rest there is unusual peace that others will not understand. You will sail through the storms unmoved and unbothered.

CONFESSION

Father, I thank You for Your perfect and complete peace. I declare that I am unmoved and unbothered by storms or adversity. I declare that I am planted and established in Your peace. I declare that all of Your promises for my life are yes and amen!

JOURNAL

What is God speaking to you about this prophetic promise?

DAY 31

UNUSUAL GLORY

Then Moses said, "I pray You, show me Your glory!"
—EXODUS 33:18

DEFINITION

Glory—The word translated "glory" in Exodus 33:18 is *kabowd*, and it is also used to mean honor, glorious, abundance, riches, splendor, dignity, reputation, and reverence.[1]

DEVOTION

The glory of God is the manifestation of His person. When glory is present, God is in the room. We were born to be glory carriers. We were created to be people of His presence.

Moses had an unusual hunger for the presence and glory of God. He sought to see the glory of the Lord, and God answered by letting His goodness pass before Moses. I believe God is releasing an unusual hunger in your spirit to see, experience, and enjoy His glory.

Unusual realms of glory will unlock uncommon miracles and breakthrough. Today is a day to cry out for unusual measures of God's glory. It is a day to seek, pursue, and ask for the glory realm. The glory realm will lift you. The glory realm will protect you. The glory realm will birth revelation in your life. The glory realm will refresh you.

I believe that unusual levels of glory have been appointed

for you. Believe for the glory! Expect the glory! Cry out for the glory!

CONFESSION

Lord, I want to see and experience Your glory. I am hungry for Your glory. I decree that I am a glory carrier. I walk in Your glory. I carry Your glory. I release Your glory in the earth. I love the glory! The glory is my portion in the name of Jesus. Amen.

JOURNAL

What is God speaking to you about this prophetic promise?

DAY 32

UNUSUAL PROPHETIC WORDS

But who has stood in the council of the LORD,
that he should see and hear His word? Who
has given heed to His word and listened?

—JEREMIAH 23:18

DEFINITION

Prophet—According to Smith's Bible Dictionary, "the ordinary Hebrew word for prophet is *nabi*, derived from a verb signifying 'to bubble forth' like a fountain; hence the word means one who announces or pours forth the declarations of God. The English word comes from the Greek *prophetes* (*profetes*), which signifies in classical Greek one who speaks for another, especially one who speaks for a god, and so interprets his will to man; hence its essential meaning is 'an interpreter.'"[1]

DEVOTION

The prophetic anointing unlocks and reveals the mind of God. It releases the wisdom and insight of the Lord. Prophets and prophetic people are called to administrate God's thoughts. They speak the heart, will, and intent of the Lord.

Prophetic words will typically require action and obedience. They can cause a seismic shift in your life. Prophetic words can abort an attack of the enemy and launch you into a new season.

Unusual prophetic words are coming to you. Words that challenge you are coming. Words that refine you are coming. Words that will require obedience are coming. One word can shift your life. Believe for unusual insight, revelation, and prophetic decree and articulation over your life. Believe for God's voice to be illuminated to you on another level.

CONFESSION

Thank You, Lord, for unusual prophetic words. I thank You that I am open to uncommon encounters, dreams, visions, mysteries, and insights. I call forth Your mind and counsel in my life, and I take all limits off. I decree that I am obedient to Your voice and will do what You tell me to do. I am not stuck, but I am in forward motion under the direction of heaven in the name of Jesus. Amen.

JOURNAL

What is God speaking to you about this prophetic promise?

DAY 33

UNUSUAL INSTRUCTIONS

So he went down and dipped himself seven times in the Jordan, according to the word of the man of God; and his flesh was restored like the flesh of a little child and he was clean.

—2 Kings 5:14

DEFINITION

Instruction—"an outline or manual of technical procedure"; "a direction calling for compliance"

DEVOTION

Naaman was a leprous leader who wanted to be healed, so he called upon a prophet who gave him extremely challenging instructions. He was told to go dip in a dirty river seven times. Naaman must have wondered why the man of God couldn't just lay his hands on him. Why couldn't he just speak forth healing? Why did Naaman have to expose his leprosy for all to see by getting into muddy waters?

These are the types of questions that arise in the human mind when God gives us unusual instructions. But if we obey God, our breakthrough is on the other side! God is looking for surrender and obedience. When Naaman did what the prophet said, he was instantly and miraculously healed. God has wonderful breakthroughs planned for you, but He will challenge you with unusual instructions. Don't shut down what you hear because it's challenging. God is waiting at the point of your obedience with your miracle.

CONFESSION

I decree that I hear, receive, and obey unusual instructions. I am not bound by human understanding alone. I am radically obedient and move forward in the things of Your Spirit, Lord. I submit myself to You today. I will follow You in Jesus' name. Amen.

JOURNAL

What is God speaking to you about this prophetic promise?

UNUSUAL OPEN DOORS

For a wide door for effective service has opened to me, and there are many adversaries.

—1 CORINTHIANS 16:9

DEFINITION

Door—"a usually swinging or sliding barrier by which an entry is closed and opened; a similar part of a piece of furniture"; "a means of access or participation"

DEVOTION

A doorway is an access point. We often pray for new seasons, assignments, and strategies, but we fail to discern the access point. It is key that we see the door and move inside of what God has for us.

We need to pray for the right doors to open. We need to claim that unusual doors of favor, opportunity, and assignment open. We need to speak forth the open doors. Doors lead to destinations.

God is causing you to stand in front of great doors. He is leading you into higher levels of function in the kingdom. He is refining you and preparing you for the great destiny He has for your life, and He will use doorways to release you into the plans and purposes He has ordained for you.

God has stunning doors for you. And not only is He

bringing you before doors, but He is going ahead of you and opening the doors. You will be placed in front of wide-open doors.

CONFESSION

Thank You, Lord, for opening the right doors in my life. I expect unusual doors of favor to open for me. I expect unusual doors of opportunity to open in my life. I expect unusual doors of blessing to open for me. I claim Your open doors in my life in the name of Jesus. Amen.

JOURNAL

What is God speaking to you about this prophetic promise?

DAY 35

UNUSUAL CLOSED DOORS

And to the angel of the church in Philadelphia write: He who is holy, who is true, who has the key of David, who opens and no one will shut, and who shuts and no one opens.

—Revelation 3:7

DEFINITION

Close—"to move so as to bar passage through something"; "to block against entry or passage"; "to deny access to"; "to suspend or stop the operations of"

DEVOTION

When we submit to the Lord, we are putting Him in charge of every aspect of our lives. We are relinquishing control. We must trust Him in His yes and trust Him in His no. He holds the power not only to cause unusual doors to open but also to close doors. As you advance in God's purposes for your life, He is going to close some unusual doors for you. This is a manifestation of His protection.

There are some seasons that will suddenly change. There are some relationships that will suddenly end. There are some assignments that will suddenly dry out. It is part of God's plan. It may look like a denial, but it is likely an act of God's protection and blessing on your life. Don't see the door closing as a punishment. See it is an answer to your prayers.

CONFESSION

God, I trust You with every assignment, relationship, and season in my life. I refuse to self-guide and self-protect. I am dependent upon You. I need You. I need Your plan for my life. I thank You for closing unusual doors. Open the right ones and close the wrong ones in my life in the name of Jesus. Amen.

JOURNAL

What is God speaking to you about this prophetic promise?

UNUSUAL ACCESS

In whom we have boldness and confident access through faith in Him.

—Ephesians 3:12

DEFINITION

Access—"permission, liberty, or ability to enter, approach, or pass to and from a place or to approach or communicate with a person or thing"; "freedom or ability to obtain or make use of something"; "a way or means of entering or approaching"; "the act or an instance of accessing something"

DEVOTION

God has given you unusual access to His plans, His ways, His love, and His glory. You are not standing outside; you are called to live in Him and move in Him. He has granted you access to every gift, every blessing, and every mantle needed to get the job done. Take your place. Be confident in the liberty that has been given to you.

Access means the ability to approach and move freely from place to place. It means the ability to obtain or make use of something. Nothing in the kingdom is blocked from you as a child of God. You need to meditate today on the access that has already been granted. You move in unusual power when you gain a revelation of the uncommon access that already belongs to you. Believe that it is yours!

CONFESSION

Father, I thank You for not withholding any good thing from me. You made a way! You cleared a path. You provided access for every plan and purpose that You have for my life. The access is mine. I take my place as Your child today. I bind the fear, shame, and condemnation that would attempt to block access. I come freely into Your presence and glory today. I thank You that access belongs to me because I am planted in You. In the name of Jesus, amen.

JOURNAL

What is God speaking to you about this prophetic promise?

UNUSUAL FREEDOM

It was for freedom that Christ set us free; therefore keep standing firm and do not be subject again to a yoke of slavery.

—GALATIANS 5:1

DEFINITION

Freedom—"the quality or state of being free: such as (a): the absence of necessity, coercion, or constraint in choice or action; (b): liberation from slavery or restraint or from the power of another; (c): the quality or state of being exempt or released usually from something onerous"

DEVOTION

Jesus came to set you totally free! People who understand and maximize the grace of God enjoy unusual freedom. They are set free from the lies of hell. They are set free from the heavy burden of religion. They are set free from guilt and condemnation. They access freedom in their minds and emotions.

Jesus didn't pay part of the price for our freedom. He laid it all on the line so that you could live in His abundant life with no restraint. Make a decision today to live in unusual freedom. Receive the overflowing love of God and His provision for every area of your life. There is no room for bondage. Jesus is the bondage breaker. When He enters a life, bondage has to flee. When He enters a room, hell has to bow. His glorious power shatters the obstructive cords of hell. Today is the day of glorious and unusual freedom for you!

CONFESSION

I declare that I am free! I am free indeed because the price for my freedom has been paid. I command all bondage to flee my life. I command fear to go. I command heaviness, doubt, shame, and worry to go. I release the life of God into every situation I face. I declare that Jesus reigns in every area of my life. I am gloriously free in the name of Jesus. Amen.

JOURNAL

What is God speaking to you about this prophetic promise?

UNUSUAL FAVOR

For it is You who blesses the righteous man, O LORD,
You surround him with favor as with a shield.

—PSALM 5:12

DEFINITION

Favor—"approving consideration or attention"; "partiality"; "permission"; "popularity"

DEVOTION

Favor opens doors and brings you before great people. Favor is God's instrument of supernatural promotion. Favor is a gift and a part of the inheritance we are to enjoy as believers. When favor manifests in your life, a promise is swiftly fulfilled. Favor will cause you to be at the right place at the right time and enjoy access. Favor will go out ahead of you.

Psalm 5:12 says favor surrounds us like a shield. That means there is a protective dimension of God's favor. The lies of the enemy have to pass through the favor on your life!

When you are surrounded by favor, you are surrounded by unusual opportunities. The force of favor will cause you to launch forward and abound. The force of favor will strip the potency of hell's words. Favor is yours; therefore, divine access and promotion are yours.

CONFESSION

I thank You, Lord, that I am surrounded by Your favor. I decree unusual levels and measures of favor upon my life, my family, my money, my job, and my assignment. Favor goes ahead of me and creates access. Favor defends me. Favor advances me. I walk in divine favor in the name of Jesus. Amen.

JOURNAL

What is God speaking to you about this prophetic promise?

UNUSUAL IDEAS

For behold, He who forms mountains and creates the wind and declares to man what are His thoughts, He who makes dawn into darkness and treads on the high places of the earth, the LORD God of hosts is His name.

—AMOS 4:13

DEFINITION

Idea—"a formulated thought or opinion"; "whatever is known or supposed about something"; "the central meaning or chief end of a particular action or situation"; "a plan for action"; "a standard of perfection"

DEVOTION

The creative power of heaven can manifest in your life though the mind of Christ. Contained within God's mind are God's ideas. What would your life look like with God's ideas abounding in your life? Great entrepreneurial efforts begin with a single idea. Profound books and intellectual properties are birthed through a single idea.

I see unusual answers and solutions coming to your life through the ideas God has for you. Begin to dream and imagine the possibilities of God. Refuse to live in the place of low thinking and limited dreaming. God did not create you to be trapped in low-level thinking. He created your mind to soar and explore His creative concepts. Your next great breakthrough can come through one flash of imagination. I see your mind aligning with heaven's rhythm. I see your thoughts coming into agreement with God's intellect. I see your imagination being set free from the prison of fear, and I see you soaring above the norm.

CONFESSION

Thank You, Lord, for Your unusual ideas, thoughts, and wisdom in my life. I decree that I have full access to Your mind and thinking. My thoughts align with Your thoughts. Your ideas are my ideas. I walk in heavenly wisdom. I see the solutions. I discern and implement Your ideas in my life. In the mighty name of Jesus, amen.

JOURNAL

What is God speaking to you about this prophetic promise?

UNUSUAL STRATEGIES

How precious also are Your thoughts to me, O God! How vast is the sum of them!

—PSALM 139:17

DEFINITION

Strategy—"the science and art of employing the political, economic, psychological, and military forces of a nation or group of nations to afford the maximum support to adopted policies in peace or war"; "the science and art of military command exercised to meet the enemy in combat under advantageous conditions"; "a variety of or instance of the use of strategy"; "a careful plan or method"; "the art of devising or employing plans or stratagems toward a goal"

DEVOTION

Strategy is the difference maker. It is the clear path taken with decisive steps to implement an idea or solution. A strategy is a manifestation of wisdom. As kingdom people we are called to be strategic people. We are called to implement solutions, but we must see, hear, and receive God's wisdom. One of the things Holy Spirit will do for us is provide strategic insight to confront and overcome challenges. Kingdom people are given a mantle to overcome. They are not supposed to stay bound.

Prophetic insight will reveal the root of the issue and the mind of God concerning a matter. If we press in, we will also receive revelation of the strategy of heaven in each situation. As prophetic people we should expect the strategy and be prepared for unusual strategy. In other words, God may show us how to do something in an unlikely fashion that challenges our natural way of thinking. Do not run from strange instructions. The strategy of the Lord may look totally different from what you expected. Obey what God says, and expect supernatural breakthrough.

CONFESSION

Father, I thank You for unusual solutions and creative strategies. I thank You for Your wisdom, which is in abundant operation in my life. I decree that I am a strategic thinker, pray-er, and seer. I am a solutionist because Your Spirit lives in me and gives me access to Your mind. I receive the strategy of heaven now in the name of Jesus. Amen.

JOURNAL

What is God speaking to you about this prophetic promise?

UNUSUAL WARFARE

The LORD is a warrior; the LORD is His name.

—EXODUS 15:3

DEFINITION

Warfare—"military operations between enemies"; "an activity undertaken by a political unit (such as a nation) to weaken or destroy another"; "economic warfare"; "struggle between competing entities: conflict"

DEVOTION

As you come into the next level of your mandate, do not be surprised if you face high levels of resistance. It is the assignment of hell to push against your progress. That is what you are facing—hell's opposition to your growth and development. It is nothing more than an evil ploy to get you to give up and quit. Do not give in.

Many times when people move up to another level of their assignment, they suddenly face attacks that are totally different from what they have experienced in the past. This is a manifestation of unusual warfare. The powers of hell are acting like guardians to oppose particular realms of truth and breakthrough. I advise people to take the warfare as a confirmation. It is confirming that you are on the right track and making progress. Instead of getting upset, start praising God! Hell sees your destiny and is trying to get you to abort it, but the Lord is a warrior. He is fighting with you and for you. You are already destined to win. He has provided unusual protection and solutions for the unusual warfare that is coming against you.

CONFESSION

Thank You, Lord, for Your power and strength in my life. I command all the lies and attacks from hell to be broken. I give You praise and glory for Your hand upon my life. I know victory is mine! I know freedom is mine! You are a warrior, and I release Your strength in every area of my life in the name of Jesus. Amen.

JOURNAL

What is God speaking to you about this prophetic promise?

DAY 42

UNUSUAL WORDS

I, the LORD, am your God, who brought you up from the land of Egypt; open your mouth wide and I will fill it.

—PSALM 81:10

DEFINITION

Word—"a speech sound or series of speech sounds that symbolizes and communicates a meaning usually without being divisible into smaller units capable of independent use"; "the entire set of linguistic forms produced by combining a single base with various inflectional elements without change in the part of speech elements"; "a written or printed character or combination of characters representing a spoken word"

DEVOTION

Language is critical in the formation of culture. Heaven has language. The Bible has language. When we get saved, our language changes.

The words we speak create in the realm of the spirit. We have the creative force of heaven on the inside of us, and our tongues are prophetic instruments of power.

God wants to give you unusual words to express and manifest His kingdom. He is going to illuminate your understanding and vocabulary. Lean in and listen! Expect Him to fill your mouth. From the midst of glory His words will come forth out of your mouth. Prophetic words will come to you. Words of wisdom will be released. You will articulate the objectives of the kingdom, and God is going to give you unusual prophetic words. Do not be afraid to speak things you have never spoken before. God is filling your mouth!

CONFESSION

Lord, I am opening my mouth and expecting You to fill it today. I receive Your creative words. I receive Your words of power. I receive expression and articulation of the kingdom. I believe that my mouth is filled with Your words today. I speak forth Your mind, Your heart, and Your power. In Jesus' name, amen.

JOURNAL

What is God speaking to you about this prophetic promise?

DAY 43

UNUSUAL SOUNDS

Yet many of the priests and Levites and heads of fathers' households, the old men who had seen the first temple, wept with a loud voice when the foundation of this house was laid before their eyes, while many shouted aloud for joy, so that the people could not distinguish the sound of the shout of joy from the sound of the weeping of the people, for the people shouted with a loud shout, and the sound was heard far away.

—EZRA 3:12–13

DEFINITION

Sound—"the sensation perceived by the sense of hearing"

DEVOTION

Heaven has sounds! There is a sound of praise. There is a sound of worship. There is a sound of hunger. I can remember preaching a number of years ago and experiencing such an unusual hunger among the people. It was clear that there was a revival flow in our midst—that God was moving. But the most amazing part was the radical pursuit of the people. They began to run to the front, seeking God. They cried, they shouted, and they prayed. The room was filled with a sound vastly different from what I had previously experienced in churches. It was not the norm. It was unusual!

Be on the lookout for unusual sounds in your life. God

may draw your ear to a prayer sound. He may highlight a worship song to you that unlocks something. Sounds create atmospheres. I believe it is the heart of God to release heaven into your life. He wants to invite you into His glory and power. Listen for the sounds of hunger and revival in your life, and then give expression to them.

CONFESSION

Father, I thank You for unusual sounds of hunger in my life. Thank You for unusual sounds of worship in my life. Thank You for unusual prophetic sounds. I decree that my spiritual ears are open and I hear Your sounds in my life in the name of Jesus. I declare that I am a worshipper and a praiser. I choose to give expression to my hunger. I choose to release the sounds of awakening in the name of Jesus. Amen.

JOURNAL

What is God speaking to you about this prophetic promise?

UNUSUAL OCCASIONS

"At the acceptable time I listened to you, and on the day of salvation I helped you." Behold, now is "the acceptable time," behold, now is "the day of salvation."

—2 CORINTHIANS 6:2

DEFINITION

Time—*kairos* in the Greek, meaning "a measure of time, a larger or smaller portion of time, hence: a fixed and definite time, the time when things are brought to crisis, the decisive epoch waited for; opportune or seasonable time; the right time; a limited period of time; to what time brings, the state of the times, the things and events of time"[1]

DEVOTION

Miracles are birthed in moments, so we must learn to discern unusual occasions. There are key windows of opportunity that we must see and seize. We cannot afford to be behind these occasions because we do not want to be out of sync with God's timing and find ourselves outside the supernatural peace of God for our lives and destiny. Miracle moments provide critical access to the dimension of divine breakthrough. It is possible to see the trajectory of your life change in a moment of time, on a single occasion.

In an unusual occasion, something that is not common

is taking place. It may be a moment of prophetic destiny or insight. It may be a moment of amazing favor. It may be a moment of restoration or healing. Determine not to run away even if you are uncomfortable in these snapshots of time. These are the answers to your prayers. Move in your moment with boldness and authority. The time is ripe with potential!

CONFESSION

God, I thank You for unusual occasions that produce healing, breakthrough, and favor in my life. I thank You for miracle moments. I thank You for divine moments. I thank You for breakthrough moments. I decree that I am moving in Your timing and that I am walking in unusual breakthrough. I see and seize my moment, in Jesus' name. Amen.

JOURNAL

What is God speaking to you about this prophetic promise?

UNUSUAL MOMENTUM

You shall walk in all the way which the LORD your God has commanded you, that you may live and that it may be well with you, and that you may prolong your days in the land which you will possess.

—DEUTERONOMY 5:33

DEFINITION

Momentum—"a property of a moving body that the body has by virtue of its mass and motion and that is equal to the product of the body's mass and velocity; *broadly*: a property of a moving body that determines the length of time required to bring it to rest when under the action of a constant force or moment"; "strength or force gained by motion or by a series of events"

DEVOTION

You were never created to be stuck. You were created to be in a state of forward motion. You were created to be moving with the rhythm of heaven for your life. You were created to advance. Demonic powers attempt to lock you in a position that heaven has not endorsed. But momentum causes things that are stuck to begin to move.

I see unusual momentum coming upon your life. God is leading you forward, and the power of hell cannot bind or restrict you. You are anointed for forward motion. If something gets stuck in the natural, it needs oil. The presence of the Holy Spirit brings the oil that provides the needed movement and causes things to break loose. Expect fresh anointing and forward motion in your life today!

CONFESSION

Father, I thank You for unusual momentum. I thank You for rapid movement in my life today. I decree that I am moving under the power of Your command. I am moving forward as You direct me. I am advancing. I decree fresh oil that causes all friction to go and divine movement to break forth in my life. In the name of Jesus, amen.

JOURNAL

What is God speaking to you about this prophetic promise?

UNUSUAL REST

For the one who has entered His rest has himself also rested from his works, as God did from His.

—HEBREWS 4:10

DEFINITION

Rest—*katapausis* in the Greek, which means "a putting to rest; calming of the winds"; "a resting place; metaph. the heavenly blessedness in which God dwells, and of which he has promised to make persevering believers in Christ partakers after the toils and trials of life on earth are ended"[1]

DEVOTION

A rested person is a peaceful person. When you are established in the peace of God, you make wise decisions and you function better. Your mind is clearer. Your body feels better. Rest is vital.

There is a natural rest, which is important, but there is also a supernatural rest that comes from God. It is a peace and refreshing far beyond human ability that comes from trusting God.

I believe God is bringing you into a place of faith that creates an unusual rest. You will no longer be overwhelmed by the struggles around you. You will no longer be trying to figure it all out on your own. You will be surrendered and trusting Him in every area. Trust creates rest. Rest produces peace, and plans and decisions born in the midst of peace are much healthier.

CONFESSION

Father, I thank You for an unusual rest in my mind. I decree that my thought life is filled with Your overwhelming peace. I decree that I think and meditate upon Your promises. I decree that my mind is planted in You. I decree that my spirit is at rest because I know that You are my Father. I decree that my life is infused with Your rest in every area. I do not strive or struggle, because I am planted in You, and You are good! I receive Your rest in my life, in the name of Jesus. Amen.

JOURNAL

What is God speaking to you about this prophetic promise?

UNUSUAL DOMINION

You make him to rule over the works of Your hands; You have put all things under his feet.

—PSALM 8:6

DEFINITION

Dominion—"domain"; "law: supreme authority: sovereignty"; "absolute ownership"

DEVOTION

Man was created in the image and likeness of God to rule and reign. It was the original plan of God for His children to represent Him with power and authority. It was only after the fall of Adam and Eve, when they relinquished their God-appointed authority, that the enemy got a foothold in the earth. Jesus came to redeem, or buy back, mankind! He came to undo what Adam and Eve did.

We are now positioned in Jesus and called to reign. We are not to bow to the powers of hell. Hell is to bow to us. We are not to run from demonic opposition. We are to break and rule over opposition through our kingdom authority.

God wants to establish you in faith for unusual dominion. He wants you to take your place of rulership in Him to defeat the works of the enemy. The victory belongs to you!

CONFESSION

Father, I thank You that I walk in Your dominion. I am not subject to the attacks of the enemy. I rule and reign in You. I soar high in You. I ride Your winds and move in Your glory. I am Your child; therefore, dominion belongs to me. I decree Your dominion in my life today. In the mighty name of Jesus, amen.

JOURNAL

What is God speaking to you about this prophetic promise?

UNUSUAL TURNAROUNDS

When He saw them, He said to them, "Go and show yourselves to the priests." And as they were going, they were cleansed.

—LUKE 17:14

DEFINITION

Turn around—(verb): "to become changed for the better"; "to act in an abrupt, different, or surprising manner"

Turnaround—(noun): "turnabout"; "a change or reversal of direction, trend, policy, role, or character"; "a changing from one allegiance to another"

DEVOTION

A turnaround is necessary to undo what has been done. How many times have we faced situations that seemed impossible to reverse? These same situations can be undone in a moment in the midst of God's power! The ten lepers that Jesus healed experienced a turnaround. (See Luke 17:11–19.) Blind Bartimaeus experienced a turnaround when Jesus restored his sight. (See Mark 10:46–52.) The woman with the issue of blood had a remarkable turnaround when Jesus made her whole. (See Luke 8:43–48.) This is what God's power does; it deactivates the power of the attack and sends it back where it originated.

Unusual turnarounds happen with ease in the presence of God. Today and moving forward, believe for your turnaround. Look over your life and identify the areas that need to turn around by God's power. They can and will change as you stand in faith. Believe the promise of God today. Give Him thanks in advance that your particular issue is going to change!

CONFESSION

Thank You, Lord, for unusual turnarounds in my life. I expect them. I believe for them. I decree the turnarounds. I decree that You are causing situations to change for the good in my life. I decree that Your power is at work. I am not afraid or discouraged. I stand upon Your Word and believe that heaven is turning every negative situation in my life around. I believe miracle power is flowing today, in the name of Jesus. Amen.

JOURNAL

What is God speaking to you about this prophetic promise?

UNUSUAL FLOW

Immediately Jesus, perceiving in Himself that the power proceeding from Him had gone forth, turned around in the crowd and said, "Who touched My garments?"

—MARK 5:30

DEFINITION

Flow—(verb): "to issue or move in a stream"; "to proceed smoothly and readily"; "to derive from a source"; (noun): "an act of flowing"; "a smooth uninterrupted movement or progress"

DEVOTION

When God's power begins to flow, unusual things take place. God's power can change a situation. It can heal a body. It can straighten out a crooked place. The flow makes the difference. An unusual flow will unlock unusual results. An unusual flow will bring much-needed strength and ability. An unusual flow will release power and breakthrough.

When the flow of heaven pours over you, your life is changed. I declare an unusual flow of God's power, grace, and glory is upon you. As it flows over you, you are being given an empowerment to do what you are called to do. Unusual virtue flows to bring life. Unusual wisdom flows from the mind of God. Unusual anointing flows to equip, strengthen, and break bondages. The unusual flow will bring you unusual results.

Get in the flow. Stay in the flow. Give God glory for the flow. There is power in the flow!

CONFESSION

Thank You, Lord, for the flow of Your power in my life. Thank You, Lord, for the flow of Your anointing in my life. Thank You, Lord, for the flow of Your favor in my life. Thank You, Lord, for the flow of Your grace in my life. I call forth Your unusual flow in my life today. I say that the river is flowing. I say that the glory is flowing. I say that wisdom is flowing. I receive Your flow in my life in Jesus' name. Amen.

JOURNAL

What is God speaking to you about this prophetic promise?

UNUSUAL ELEVATION

The LORD makes poor and rich; He brings low, He also exalts. He raises the poor from the dust, He lifts the needy from the ash heap to make them sit with nobles, and inherit a seat of honor; for the pillars of the earth are the LORD'S, and He set the world on them.

—1 SAMUEL 2:7–8

DEFINITION

Elevation—"the height to which something is elevated: such as (a): the angular distance of something (such as a celestial object) above the horizon, (b): the degree to which a gun is aimed above the horizon, (c): the height above the level of the sea"; "the ability to achieve an elevation"; "an act or instance of elevating"; "something that is elevated"; "the quality or state of being elevated"

DEVOTION

It is God who promotes and exalts! It is He who can place you in a position others have tried to obtain. You can end up there simply because you pleased Him. When God exalts you, no one can knock you out of the place where He establishes you. He causes the winds of promotion to blow upon your life.

Unusual elevation comes from the Lord. He creates avenues of opportunity for you. He places His people in positions of influence and favor to make an impact for the kingdom. This is the manifestation of the kingdom. It is vital that we understand that elevation comes from Him for a purpose. We are elevated to establish righteousness and to do the work of the kingdom.

CONFESSION

Thank You, Lord, for Your elevation in my life. I decree that You are lifting and establishing me into divine position. I thank You that I walk in humility. I recognize that elevation and favor are Your doing and not my own. I receive Your elevation in the name of Jesus. Amen.

JOURNAL

What is God speaking to you about this prophetic promise?

UNUSUAL RELEASE

And it shall come to pass in that day, that his burden shall be taken away from off thy shoulder, and his yoke from off thy neck, and the yoke shall be destroyed because of the anointing.

—Isaiah 10:27, KJV

DEFINITION

Release—"to set free from restraint, confinement, or servitude"; "to relieve from something that confines, burdens, or oppresses"; "to move from one's normal position"

DEVOTION

The Lord has an unusual release for you. It is time for you to be cut loose from burdensome confinement. Under the power of an unusual release something breaks loose. There is strategic movement in a person's life.

Not only does God want to release you, but He also wants to release things that concern you. Imagine God releasing things that have been held up—ideas being released, monies being released, prophetic strategies being released. Heaven has unusual releases for you!

When you are released, you are moved from your normal position. This means that you are moved into something new. Most of the time when God is leading you into a place of breakthrough, it is going to require a change of operation and position. This demands an unusual release!

CONFESSION

Father, I thank You that unusual release is upon me. I am being divinely shifted into my right position. Things are being released for my good and my favor. I decree a release of ideas, funds, assignments, and opportunities. Everything that has been delayed that belongs to me must be released now in the name of Jesus. I decree that I am released from all entanglements and that I am free to navigate and enjoy Your will. In Jesus' name, amen.

JOURNAL

What is God speaking to you about this prophetic promise?

UNUSUAL SEED

Solomon went up there before the* L*ORD to the bronze altar which was at the tent of meeting, and offered a thousand burnt offerings on it.

—2 CHRONICLES 1:6

DEFINITION

Seed—"the grains or ripened ovules of plants used for sowing"; "the fertilized ripened ovule of a flowering plant containing an embryo and capable normally of germination to produce a new plant"; "the condition or stage of bearing seed"; "a source of development or growth"

DEVOTION

Before he prayed for wisdom, Solomon offered a thousand burnt offerings on an altar built for only one offering at a time. He offered an unusual seed, and God answered him in an unusual way by giving him abundant wisdom and riches. Solomon's seed provoked God.

There are realms of giving that will break you through into new dimensions of harvest. Most of the time you will feel nervous or even afraid to give at that level, but as you press past that test, you will crack the glass ceiling over your life.

Unusual seeds begin with an unusual prompting. You will sense God tugging at you to do it. You will experience a peaceful assurance, and on the other side of your obedience will be a tremendous breakthrough.

God never challenges you to give because He desires to take something from you. He is looking to add to your life. Giving is an act of kingdom living. Kingdom people are givers. Your money is not your only seed. Your time, your service, and your prayers are seeds. Your entire life is a seed. God will lead you to release unusual seeds in order to bring you into levels and measures of unusual receiving.

CONFESSION

I decree that I sow unusual seeds and reap unusual harvests. I decree that abundance is mine in the name of Jesus. I declare that I am sensitive to Your Spirit, Lord. When You speak to me about sowing, I am not afraid. I do not rebel, nor do I withhold from You. I release what You tell me to give, and I anticipate an unusual, supernatural harvest in the name of Jesus. Amen.

JOURNAL

What is God speaking to you about this prophetic promise?

UNUSUAL DISCOVERY

It is the glory of God to conceal a matter, but the glory of kings is to search out a matter.

—Proverbs 25:2

DEFINITION

Discover—"to make known or visible"; "to obtain sight or knowledge of for the first time: find"; "to make a discovery"

DEVOTION

Discovery in this context is a prophetic act. It is to look into the realm of the spirit and find what was previously hidden. This is a major key to living in the will of God for your life. You cannot navigate what you have not sought out and discovered.

The Lord is releasing unusual discovery as you lean into Him. He is going to cause you to find the solution. He is going to cause you to see the next step. He is going to cause the hidden to be revealed. He is going to allow the light to shine on what has been shrouded. This is part of His plan for your increase and provision. It is part of His divine mind toward you. He is releasing the ability to find something out, to see it, and to know it. This is your portion as His child!

CONFESSION

Thank You, Lord, for the unusual discoveries in my life. I decree that the spirit of wisdom and revelation is active inside me. I say that my spiritual eyes are sharp and my ears hear well. I am led by Your Spirit into all truth, including Your divine will for my life. Nothing is hidden from me that You have intended for me to see and know. I clearly know Your will. I clearly know Your heart. I am Your child, and I decree that I rightly discern Your thoughts. In the name of Jesus, amen.

JOURNAL

What is God speaking to you about this prophetic promise?

UNUSUAL TRUST

And those who know Your name will put their trust in You, for You, O LORD, have not forsaken those who seek You.
—PSALM 9:10

DEFINITION

Trust—"assured reliance on the character, ability, strength, or truth of someone or something"; "one in which confidence is placed"; "dependence on something future or contingent: hope"

DEVOTION

The Father has you on a pathway not only of pursuit but also of trust. He is teaching you how to have confidence in His plans, His ways, and His will for your life. Your mind will try to figure it all out, but sometimes the moment just demands a leap of faith. That is the key to the breakthrough: bold faith in God.

The life of a person who trusts God is one of peace and pursuit. As you become fully aware of the love the Father has for you, you develop a mentality of unusual trust. You are willing to pursue difficult instructions that defy logic. You are willing to do as Peter did in Luke 5 and launch out into the deep, even when your brain is screaming, "No way!" It's on the other side of acting in faith because of your trust in

God that you see the greatest realm of harvest. Those who dare to trust God in an audacious fashion reap huge benefits.

CONFESSION

Lord, I trust You. I have confidence in You. I believe that when You speak, it is for my good. I believe that when You lead, You have a blessing in mind. I am not afraid to step out and obey You. I decree and declare that I live free from fear. I decree that I live in the realm of unusual trust and confidence in You. In the name of Jesus, amen.

JOURNAL

What is God speaking to you about this prophetic promise?

UNUSUAL CATAPULT

When He had finished speaking, He said to Simon, "Put out into the deep water and let down your nets for a catch."
—LUKE 5:4

DEFINITION

Catapult—(verb): "to throw or launch by or as if by a catapult"; (noun): "an ancient military device for hurling missiles"

DEVOTION

A heavenly catapult will cause you to suddenly and swiftly break forth. It is time for you to break forth into heavenly plans and assignments. It is time for your health to break forth. It is time for opportunities and appointments to break forth. It is time for uncommon wisdom to break forth.

When the unusual catapult hits your life, you are propelled toward the answer! There is nothing like heaven's answers and solutions for your life. Be aware that there is supernatural timing connected to every prophetic promise in your life.

The enemy will attempt to attack your faith. He will tell you the thing that God said is not going to happen, but he is an absolute fraud and liar (John 8:44). Do not give in to his voice. You are being prepared for the catapult. If you keep obeying God, He will shift you in a moment of time, and the enemy will not be able to stop it.

CONFESSION

Father, I thank You for divine liftoff in my life. I decree rapid forward motion. I declare an unusual catapulting of my life in the name of Jesus. I decree that God's liftoff is working in me and for me. I declare that I am launched forward by the power of God into every blessing and purpose that belongs to me in the name of Jesus! Amen.

JOURNAL

What is God speaking to you about this prophetic promise?

UNUSUAL FAMILY BREAKTHROUGHS

Behold, I and the children whom the LORD has given me are for signs and wonders in Israel from the LORD of hosts, who dwells on Mount Zion.

—ISAIAH 8:18

DEFINITION

Breakthrough—"warfare: an offensive military assault that penetrates and carries beyond a defensive line"; "an act or instance of moving through or beyond an obstacle"; "a sudden advance especially in knowledge or technique" (i.e., "a medical breakthrough"); "a person's first notable success"

DEVOTION

Before God ever created a church, He formed a family. Family is His plan. He has ordained families to worship Him, seek Him, and walk in their spiritual inheritance as His children. When you get saved, you become a conduit for the blessing and the purposes of God for your family. You may be the only one who knows certain truths about the kingdom. God has positioned you as a bloodline breaker to release your entire family into His plans.

Become an intercessor and refuse to accept anything less than God's best for your family. He has made a covenant with you that includes your family. He wants to use you to stand in the gap for your loved ones. He wants you to grab hold of His word and claim it for every family member, then rest in Him and worship Him.

Thank God today for unusual family breakthroughs. Angels are being dispatched as you pray. Glory is being released as you pray. Victory is being seized as you pray. Believe and look for the breakthrough. It belongs to you!

CONFESSION

As for me and my house, we will serve the Lord! Father, I thank You for Your promises for my family. I thank You that Your Word is truth. I claim salvation for every member of my bloodline. I claim miracles and deliverance for my family. I bind the powers of hell and loose the blood of Jesus over my family. I decree miraculous breakthroughs for my family in the name of Jesus. Amen.

JOURNAL

What is God speaking to you about this prophetic promise?

UNUSUAL FRIENDS

He who walks with wise men will be wise, but the companion of fools will suffer harm.

—PROVERBS 13:20

DEFINITION

Friend—*ra`ah*, the Hebrew word translated "companion" in Proverbs 13:20, means "to associate with, be a friend of (meaning probable); (Qal) to associate with; (Hithpael) to be companions"[1]

DEVOTION

One of the greatest gifts that God can give you is good friends. I believe He is sending unusual and supernatural relationships to your life—friends who will bless you and not stress you. He is bringing healthy people into your life who will be a part of His plan for you and not just sap all the energy out of you.

Many people are drained because they hang out with the wrong people. They spend all their time around people who love drama and create toxic atmospheres. Give yourself permission to be free of those who add excessive and continual burdens to your life. Be free of their manipulation. Be free of their demands. Be free of their unhealthy emotions. Do not live in a false sense of responsibility for people to whom you owe nothing except to love them. Cooperate with what God wants to do in your relationships, and get the right friends in your life!

CONFESSION

Father, I thank You for putting good friends in my life. I thank You for unusual friendships that bless me, challenge me, and lead me deeper into You. Set me free from negative people, doubters, and complainers. Remove the wrong people and send the right people into my life in Jesus' name. Amen.

JOURNAL

What is God speaking to you about this prophetic promise?

DAY 58

UNUSUAL SURRENDER

For in Him we live and move and exist, as even some of your own poets have said, "For we also are His children."

—ACTS 17:28

DEFINITION

Surrender—"to yield to the power, control, or possession of another upon compulsion or demand"; "to give up completely or agree to forgo especially in favor of another"; "to give (oneself) up into the power of another especially as a prisoner"; "to give (oneself) over to something (such as an influence)"

DEVOTION

The altar is the place of refining. It is the place where our hearts submit fully to the will of God. In many ways it is a place of death but also of resurrection. Our surrender invites new levels of God's glory and grace to flow in us and through us. When we lay it all down, His resurrection power comes alive inside us.

There is a call upon each of us to live a life of unusual surrender. When we surrender, we are demonstrating full obedience and reliance on the Father. It is in that place of absolute dependence that our hearts take flight as His power meets our yes! Pray today for a greater level of surrender.

Believe today to live a life planted in Him. As you lay it all down, His glory will rise.

CONFESSION

Here I am, Lord. Use me! I submit to Your ways, Your plan, and Your will for my life. I choose to live planted in You. I lay it all down. I want You. I want Your ways. I want Your will. I want Your agenda. I want to move in You. I want to be operating under Your grace and thriving through Your power in the name of Jesus. Amen.

JOURNAL

What is God speaking to you about this prophetic promise?

UNUSUAL PLANTING

For the one who sows to his own flesh will from the flesh reap corruption, but the one who sows to the Spirit will from the Spirit reap eternal life.

—GALATIANS 6:8

DEFINITION

Plant—"to put or set in the ground for growth"; "to set or sow with seeds or plants"; "implant"; "establish, institute"; "colonize, settle"

DEVOTION

What are you planting today? This question is important to consider because your life is the sum total of what you have sown and for what you have believed. This isn't my opinion; it is a kingdom principle. We are living in perpetual sowing and reaping.

We must be intentional about planting into the realm of the spirit. Unusual growth requires unusual planting. The harvest we receive is the result of what we plant. When we see someone operating in miraculous power, we are seeing the result of what that person has planted. When we see a person with godly character or discipline, we are witnessing a surrendered life. When we see a person lifted out of obscurity and raised up in a miraculous way for a kingdom purpose, we are typically witnessing the result of his or her harvest.

Plant today for where you want to be tomorrow. Pray with destiny in mind. Sow with the harvest in mind. Build with breakthrough in mind. Focus on planting the proper seeds.

CONFESSION

Father, I thank You that I am a kingdom planter. I sow into the realm of the spirit. I decree that I am an unusual sower, and I expect an unusual, supernatural harvest. I decree that I see the opportunity to sow and move in obedience. I sow without fear or limitation. I sow by faith, and I grow by faith in Jesus' name. Amen.

JOURNAL

What is God speaking to you about this prophetic promise?

UNUSUAL ADVENTURES

But the people that do know their God
shall be strong, and do exploits.

—Daniel 11:32, KJV

DEFINITION

Adventure—"an undertaking usually involving danger and unknown risks"; "the encountering of risks"; "an exciting or remarkable experience"

DEVOTION

Serving God is a great adventure. As you grow and mature in God, you are invited to step out into uncommon realms of faith and breakthrough. His voice urges you deeper. If you trust Him, you move with Him and live free of fear. Freedom from fear is your portion!

Unusual adventures have been appointed for you. There are assignments coming that you did not see. There are miracles awaiting your obedience and discovery. There are exploits with your name on them. The realm of adventure is not for the timid but for the brave. As you lean into the Father, He is marking your heart with confidence. He is establishing you firmly in faith so that you can enjoy the journey deep into the unknown. It is in that place of wild abandon that you find realms of His power, realms you have not previously experienced. He is urging you to go for it! Be daring! The breakthrough is on the other side of your yes.

CONFESSION

Father, I thank You for this unusual journey. I believe that You are commissioning me for breakthroughs, miracles, and adventures in You. I decree that I am delivered from fear. I decree that I hear and obey when You speak. I decree that I am willing to do what You say. I decree that I am mantled with the spirit of faith. I will go where You say. I will do what You tell me. I will rise to the challenge, and I will embark upon exploits by Your power in Jesus' name. Amen.

JOURNAL

What is God speaking to you about this prophetic promise?

CONCLUSION

God is connecting people for unusual purpose. He is forming coalitions, tribes, and families, and people are cross-pollinating from various streams. The walls are coming down so that the kingdom can advance.

Expect the unusual in your life!

- Unusual glory
- Unusual miracles
- Unusual assignments
- Unusual favor
- Unusual blessings
- Unusual contracts
- Unusual partnerships, connections, and alignments
- Unusual prophetic words
- Unusual instructions
- Unusual gatherings
- Unusual breakthrough
- Unusual benefactors
- Unusual cleansing
- Unusual doorways and dimensions
- Unusual revelation
- Unusual ideas
- Unusual creative properties
- Unusual investments
- Unusual churches, teams, and ministries
- Unusual warfare
- Unusual protection
- Unusual books written
- Unusual angelic activity

- Unusual operations in the spirit realm
- Unusual healings and creative miracles
- Unusual lyrics and melodies
- Unusual songs
- Unusual sounds
- Unusual manifestations of heaven on earth
- Unusual psalmists
- Unusual moments
- Unusual prophetic words
- Unusual protection
- Unusual *shamar*
- Unusual discerning of spirits
- Unusual insight
- Unusual praise
- Unusual dancing
- Unusual rejoicing
- Unusual celebration
- Unusual creativity
- Unusual genius
- Unusual concepts
- Unusual events
- Unusual endeavors
- Unusual cleansing
- Unusual separation
- Unusual disconnects
- Unusual blockage (God blocking the wrong doors)
- Unusual prayer
- Unusual seeking
- Unusual hunger
- Unusual tenacity
- Unusual grace
- Unusual compassion
- Unusual mercy
- Unusual reconciliation
- Unusual mending
- Unusual relational healing
- Unusual salvation
- Unusual leading
- Unusual study
- Unusual reading
- Unusual meditation
- Unusual decrees

- Unusual drawing
- Unusual stability
- Unusual determination
- Unusual stamina
- Unusual peace
- Unusual tranquility
- Unusual refreshing
- Unusual boldness
- Unusual confrontation
- Unusual dominion
- Unusual authority
- Unusual faith
- Unusual instant turnarounds
- Unusual release of anointing
- Unusual bursting forth
- Unusual eruptions
- Unusual breaking loose
- Unusual tearing down walls
- Unusual release of captives
- Unusual breaker anointing
- Unusual drop of heavy glory
- Unusual interruptions of gatherings
- Unusual and sudden encounters
- Unusual and breath-taking experiences

This word is for you. This word is for now. This word is setting the bar for God plans, God breakthroughs, and God adventures. The unusual is your portion!

NOTES

INTRODUCTION

1. *Merriam-Webster* (thesaurus), s.v. "unusual," accessed September 10, 2019, https://www.merriam-webster.com/thesaurus/unusual.

DAY 3

1. Blue Letter Bible, s.v. "*chriō*," accessed September 10, 2019, https://www.blueletterbible.org/lang/Lexicon/Lexicon.cfm?strongs=G5548&t=KJV.

DAY 11

1. Blue Letter Bible, s.v. "*shamar*," accessed September 10, 2019, https://www.blueletterbible.org/lang/Lexicon/Lexicon.cfm?strongs=H8104&t=KJV.
2. John Eckhardt, *The Prophet's Manual* (Lake Mary, FL: Charisma House, 2017), 134; *Merriam-Webster*, s.v. "guard," accessed September 10, 2019, https://www.merriam-webster.com/dictionary/guard.

DAY 12

1. *Merriam-Webster*, s.v. "insight," accessed September 10, 2019, https://www.merriam-webster.com/dictionary/insight.
2. Google Dictionary, s.v. "insight," accessed September 10, 2019, http://googledictionary.freecollocation.com/meaning?word=insight.
3. Christine A. Lindberg, ed., *Oxford American Writer's Thesaurus*, 3rd ed. (New York: Oxford University Press, 2012), 476.

DAY 16

1. *Merriam-Webster*, s.v. "seek," accessed September 10, 2019, https://www.merriam-webster.com/dictionary/seek.
2. Dictionary.com, s.v. "seek," accessed September 10, 2019, https://www.dictionary.com/browse/seek.

DAY 18

1. Blue Letter Bible, s.v. "*shachah*," accessed September 10, 2019, https://www.blueletterbible.org/lang/Lexicon/Lexicon.cfm?strongs=H7812&t=KJV.

DAY 19

1. Dr. Roger Barrier, "8 Hebrew Words for 'Praise' Every Christian Needs to Know," Crosswalk.com, accessed September 10, 2019, https://www.crosswalk.com/faith/spiritual-life/8-hebrew-words-for-praise-every-christian-needs-to-know.html.
2. Blue Letter Bible, s.v. "*halal*," accessed September 10, 2019, https://www.blueletterbible.org/lang/Lexicon/Lexicon.cfm?strongs=H1984&t=KJV.
3. Blue Letter Bible, s.v. "*yadah*," accessed September 10, 2019, https://www.blueletterbible.org/lang/Lexicon/Lexicon.cfm?strongs=H3034&t=KJV.
4. Blue Letter Bible, s.v. "*barak*," accessed September 10, 2019, https://www.blueletterbible.org/lang/Lexicon/Lexicon.cfm?strongs=H1288&t=KJV.
5. Blue Letter Bible, s.v. "*tĕhillah*," accessed September 10, 2019, https://www.blueletterbible.org/lang/Lexicon/Lexicon.cfm?strongs=H8416&t=KJV.
6. Blue Letter Bible, s.v. "*zamar*," accessed September 10, 2019, https://www.blueletterbible.org/lang/Lexicon/Lexicon.cfm?strongs=H2167&t=KJV.
7. Blue Letter Bible, s.v. "*towdah*," accessed September 10, 2019, https://www.blueletterbible.org/lang/Lexicon/Lexicon.cfm?strongs=H8426&t=KJV.
8. Blue Letter Bible, s.v. "*shabach*," accessed September 10, 2019, https://www.blueletterbible.org/lang/Lexicon/Lexicon.cfm?strongs=H7623&t=KJV.

DAY 20

1. "What Is the Meaning of *Exousia* in the Bible?" Got Questions Ministries, July 26, 2019, https://www.gotquestions.org/exousia-meaning.html; Blue Letter Bible, s.v. "*exousia*,"

accessed September 10, 2019, https://www.blueletterbible.org/lang/Lexicon/Lexicon.cfm?strongs=G1849&t=KJV.

DAY 21

1. Lexico.com, s.v. "stamina," accessed September 10, 2019, https://www.lexico.com/en/definition/stamina.

DAY 22

1. *Random House Kernerman Webster's College Dictionary* (2010), s.v. "atmosphere," accessed September 10, 2019, https://www.thefreedictionary.com/Atmosfer.

DAY 26

1. Google Dictionary, s.v. "restore," accessed September 10, 2019, http://googledictionary.freecollocation.com/meaning?word=restore.

DAY 28

1. Blue Letter Bible, s.v. "*krinō*," accessed September 10, 2019, https://www.blueletterbible.org/lang/Lexicon/Lexicon.cfm?strongs=G2919&t=KJV.

DAY 29

1. *Merriam-Webster (thesaurus)*, s.v. "expect," accessed September 10, 2019, https://www.merriam-webster.com/thesaurus/expect.

DAY 30

1. Blue Letter Bible, s.v. "*shalowm*," accessed September 10, 2019, https://www.blueletterbible.org/lang/Lexicon/Lexicon.cfm?strongs=H7965&t=KJV; Blue Letter Bible, s.v. "*shalam*," accessed September 10, 2019, https://www.blueletterbible.org/lang/Lexicon/lexicon.cfm?strongs=H7999&t=KJV.

DAY 31

1. Blue Letter Bible, s.v. "*kabowd*," accessed September 10, 2019, https://www.blueletterbible.org/lang/Lexicon/Lexicon.cfm?strongs=H3519&t=KJV.

DAY 32

1. Bible Study Tools, s.v. "prophet," accessed September 10, 2019, https://www.biblestudytools.com/dictionaries/smiths-bible-dictionary/prophet.html.

DAY 44

1. Blue Letter Bible, s.v. "*kairos*," accessed September 10, 2019, https://www.blueletterbible.org/lang/Lexicon/Lexicon.cfm?strongs=G2540&t=KJV.

DAY 46

1. Blue Letter Bible, s.v. "*katapausis*," accessed September 10, 2019, https://www.blueletterbible.org/lang/Lexicon/Lexicon.cfm?strongs=G2663&t=KJV.

DAY 57

1. Blue Letter Bible, s.v. "*ra`ah*," accessed September 10, 2019, https://www.blueletterbible.org/lang/Lexicon/Lexicon.cfm?strongs=H7462&t=KJV.

Ryan LeStrange is an apostolic and prophetic revolutionary, laboring to see global awakening. He moves strongly in the power of God traveling the globe to ignite revival fires and build a growing apostolic-prophetic movement. His conferences and gatherings are alive with prophetic declaration, miracles and healings, fire, and powerful preaching.

Ryan is the founder and apostolic leader of a global network of ministries known as TRIBE Network. He is a cofounder of AwakeningTV.com, a media channel created to host revival-inspired services featuring ministers and messages both past and present. He is the senior leader of the iHub movement, planting and overseeing a network of governing churches, apostolic hubs, and revival hubs. Ryan is also a real estate investor, active in the business arena.

Ryan is a best-selling author. His books include ***Supernatural Access, Overcoming Spiritual Attack, Releasing the Prophetic,*** and ***Revival Hubs Rising,*** which was coauthored with Jennifer LeClaire.

Ryan and his wife, Joy, have one son, Joshua, and currently reside in Virginia.

INVITE RYAN @ ryanlestrange.com

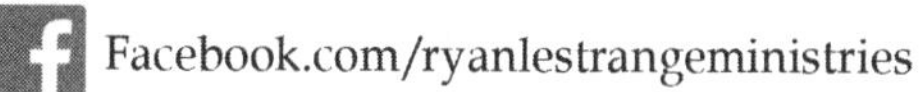